Passionistas Talk!
The Best of
The Passion Point
Interviews

By Caren Glasser
and Friends

Published by:
PYP Publishing Group
Address: 11 Valley Club Circle
City, State Zip: Napa, CA 94558
For Further information please visit www.PYPPublishingGroup.com or call: 415-599-4475

Passionistas Talk - The Best of *The Passion Point* Interviews
©2013 Caren Glasser
All rights reserved.

Cover Design and Editor: Jaqueline Kyle
PYP Publishing Group
www.PYPPublishingGroup.com
First Printing: 2013
ISBN: 0991041623

Table of Contents

Welcome Reader!

This book, Passionista's Talk! has been the culmination of an incredible journey for me. I started a series of nationwide speaking events called Promote Your Passion to create a nurturing environment for entrepreneurs. These events helped thousands to find their passion and purpose and created a community of self-proclaimed "passionistas."

The feedback was incredible but many people were not able to travel to our events. To spread the message and continue to inspire our existing passionistas I created a show called The Passion Point. It is a weekly talk show with each week featuring a different, talented passionista discussing their journey to self-fulfillment. Each guest is passionate about what they do and is successful in pursuing a career in their field of choice.

What follows is eight incredible women and four hours of interviews transcribed into book format. My hope for you is that you are inspired by the women in these interviews. Some have faced enormous challenges and have thrived in spite of or because of those challenges. Some have taken a chance on themselves with no one else to say, "You can do it." All have had doubts and fears and pressed on even though it would have been easier to quit.

I hope that you are as inspired by them as I am.

This book is meant for you to enjoy their messages at your own pace and take their lessons to heart. Each of us learns in a different way, and for some, the written word is best. May their inspiration light a passion within you.

Your Chief Passionista,

Caren Glasser

KATHY STOVER

JANUARY 10, 2013

CG: Hello everyone, Caren Glasser here and welcome to *The Passion Point*. This is the show that invites some of the top passionistas in the world to share their passion and how they are making a living doing what they love. I am really excited today because our guest is Kathy Stover. She is hands-down, one of the best, and prolific, social media strategists that I have ever had the pleasure to meet. She is the one you call when you want to grow your online reputation and online revenue. She's the one that knows how to take what your graphic artist designs, what your IT guy programs, and all of the fans your Facebook guru got you, and turns them into real revenue. Pretty cool Kathy, I actually went and read your bio and stuff.

KS: *(laughs)*

CG: You were probably wondering how I knew all that.

KS: I was going, "WOW!"

CG: Well you need a Kathy Stover on your team, there is no question about that. I know that, I mean Kathy and I have known each other for a couple of years but it's only been recently that we've had a chance to really get to know one another. And you definitely need a Kathy Stover on your team. I am just so honored to call you a friend and I'm really excited that you are on the show. We're going to talk about YOU, all about you today, and how you followed your passion. So welcome to the show, Kathy.

KS: Caren, thank you so much. I am as honored and excited to be here with you and I am honored as well to call you my friend. We have had such fun times and I'm excited to share with everybody... Passion!

CG: Woo Hoo! So I always start the show by just repeating the definition that *Websters Dictionary* has for the word passion. It says, "An intense driving, or overmastering feeling or conviction." So, how would you define passion?

KS: How would I define passion? It is so many different things. You just shared the *Webster's Dictionary* definition, but passion is different to so many people and for me I think it is who you are and what you do naturally. I think that part of it, part of the passion in us, is what we share and what energizes the people around us.

CG: So true. And as you said, passion means different things to different people. I like to say it's what gets you up in the morning. What is it that just makes you jump out of bed and want to go do what you are doing. That's sort of how I, in my own head, wrap my head around that. If you want to get out of bed to go do it, you must be passionate about it. It's got to be something that wants to get you out of bed. For many people, it's an overused word, used too often, but what is your view on passion?

KS: Interesting that you bring that up because I recently read an article about that. "Purpose" and "passion" and how it can be overused. I think the platform, Caren, that you have brought in particular, is fantastic. You have brought together so many men and women and allowed them to share their individual passion and what it means to them personally. I think that passion has been overused in some instances, but I feel it's a core emotional feeling. It has a lot to do with alignment, who we are and the energy that comes from it. I think that passion comes from many different avenues in our lives. Sometimes it can be related sexually. Sometimes it can be related in the jobs that we do or the people that we connect with. Our children. Many, many things. So it boils down to the basic emotion and desire that we have to be in alignment with the energy of it.

CG: So the question begs to be asked… What is your passion?

KS: You know I am very passionate about many things. When I talk to clients of mine, and we talk about the difference between purpose and passion, one thing that I talk about is that we can be passionate about so many things. If we are on purpose, that is focused and that's the main thing that our calling or our gifting is. So when you ask me what I am passionate about, I am very passionate about helping others, about putting smiles on other people's faces, sharing myself and my gifts and my talents with other people. I'm passionate about my grandchildren. I have three grandchildren, and just seeing them and what they have going on in their lives. I'm passionate about the fact that what I am doing in my life is creating a legacy for my grandchildren. That just thrills me and fills me. I am passionate about the connections I make and the friends that I have. Just the interchange with the people around me. So… I am passionate about LOTS of things!

CG: That's awesome. The first thing you mentioned is that you are passionate about helping people. So how did you discover that, how did you stumble upon that? Is it nature or nurture? Did you wake up one

5

day and say "I want to help people!" or did you have this feeling since you were a child? How did you come upon this passion to help people?

KS: I think it does stem from when I was a child. I was the oldest of five kids and often I would play the role of mom through some of the years. I was always for the underdog. If you can picture this, back when I was in the third or fourth grade, if I saw kids or boys, picking on other boys or girls, I would actually take off my shoes, run them down and beat the… *tarnation*… out of them. (*laughs*)

I had to come up with the right word there. I have just been that way my whole life, just looking out for other people, nurturing them, caring for them. So I think it's just a part of who I am, in the fiber of my being, if you will.

CG: So how does that manifest itself today in what you are doing, in terms of helping people? Tell us about what you do, and why I call you the best social media strategist. I know that's just me, but I know that there are a lot of people who have that same feeling about you. You also do internet TV, you do a lot of different things, so tell us a little about what you do and how that helps you serve others.

KS: What I did in the corporate world for 25 years and manifesting into what I'm doing online, and have been for 10 years this year, it was all in the way of marketing. When twitter came along and I was enamored with that, and that's how it all started for me. It sort of transcended my sales and marketing background into what I'm doing today. I've always had a real heart of service and helping people and what I am doing now isn't necessarily the norm.

What differentiates me from most is the fact that I have the ability to put authors, speakers, and transformational leaders in front of massive audiences, using social media platforms using my strategy platforms that I have developed. I also use internet TV, much like what you have going on here. Love the technology. The other thing is that I have an innate ability to actually go into somebody's business and take a look at what they have going on. I listen to where they want to go and what their expectations are, and then put it all together with the technology we have to create a win-win situation for people.

CG: So it is sort of like helping people with their passion and their purpose so they can make a living doing what they love.

KS: I love how you put things with a bow on top. Yes, exactly. That is what I do.

CG: What is your favorite social media tool today?

KS: I have quite an arsenal, as you know, but I think of recent developments, I'm going to call it a tool, is DNET. DnetTV.com. It is actually a vibrant, robust tool. I am utilizing that in conjunction with some of the tricks I have up my sleeves to promote and put people out there using all of the social media outlets available. That's my #1 because it's my newest as of late.

CG: It's really cool because you are able to use other social media delivery systems with this. For instance, this show that we are doing right now, we are going to blog about it. We are going to share it out to all of the social media outlets. We are going to share it on pinterest so that it can be seen. It's great to be able to use all of these things, grabbing them from here and from there and putting it all together onto one platform. Very cool.

So what would you tell someone who is lost and is trying to get their mojo back, to get back on the right road?

KS: I think it is interesting because, as I mentioned earlier, people get muddied between passion and person. I would tell them that they need

7

to sit and truly listen to their heart. I am one of those "shiny object, it must be my passion because it is tripping my trigger," and those things can thwart it. People need to just sit and listen to their heart and their intuition and their gut.

If you are in the position right now that you're not bringing in the revenue you expected or wanted, so you are looking for things outside of what your true purpose or passion is… you are going to end up going down the wrong road and spending a lot of time and energy. If you just sit and listen to your heart, and know that the gifts and talents that you have been given are valuable, you are valuable, you have worth. Sit with that. Because that is going to be in alignment with what your true passion and your true purpose is and that will take you a long way. So just listen to your heart and your intuition.

CG: We had this conversation yesterday. I was talking about something you were doing and I was thinking of dabbling in that. But it was very important for me that if I was going to go in that direction, that it still had to fit within my wheelhouse. That it would fit into my passion. Which is why what you are saying is so important. It may be a shiny object and in its current configuration, it may not be the right thing for you, but if there is a way that you can take that shiny object and have it fit into what you are passionate about, then that is what makes a really pretty package. Do you agree?

KS: Yes. And I think the other thing is, whatever people's spiritual beliefs are, they need to sit with that. Whether it be praying and meditation, which to me is the same thing. Whatever it is that you need to do to connect, connect with your core self first, so that you know you can listen to what your heart is whispering. You'll certainly go in the right direction. There are so many shiny objects out there. As I mentioned at the onset of the show, I am into affiliated marketing as well. Let me tell you that there is all kinds of stuff coming out all of the time. It can be very easy to get off of the intended, beaten path, so to speak.

CG: And I think also… We talk about that blue ocean of abundance rather than the red sea of scarcity and when we are in a place of picking things to do because we are in that red sea of scarcity, and our thoughts are of "how am I going to pay the bills, how am I going to get through this next day," our brain focuses and thinks about and manifests the things that we think about. So if we are constantly thinking those "how am I going to get through the next day" thoughts, rather than the projects and things that we are doing to bring about an end result. Our brain is going to focus on those things that we focus on.

KS: Yes.

CG: I know you do things such as affirmations. Do you want to talk about that and how that has helped to focus your passion?

KS: I do, and that was actually a gifting from our mutual friend Linda P. Jones, America's wealth mentor. I want to give her a great plug. I have always been very spiritually connected, since I was a small child. I have always been prayerful; I've always had a very deep faith. They talk about the "light at the end of the tunnel," and I've always had the gift to see the light beyond the light at the end of the tunnel, and I am very grateful for that. With that being said, when it comes down to affirmations, they are very connected to my prayer life.

I have five affirmations that I have in my daily repertoire. When I am very cognizant of waking in the morning, there are two that I say all the time and three that I change up. And as I said, I interlace that with my prayer time as well. And I do that when I doze off and go to sleep at night as well. It has been very effective for me, being connective like that. So much so that there are times when I am sitting in my home office working, I will write something, I will start praying and meditating on it, but it is an affirmation that I set. And it actually transpires. Here is the wonderful thing, and the gifting in that for me, it's not something

9

that I share for myself. I say affirmations and prayers for others as well. It is not something that I keep only for me. I share.

CG: For those of you who are listening and thinking "Oh right, you're supposed to just think it and it's going to happen," no, that is not how it works. It's a piece of the puzzle. You still have to do the work. But I like to say that if you don't even know what you want, how are you going to know when it shows up? Right? You have to have those thoughts in your head so that when it does show up, and you are sitting in your office and you're doing something and you get a call and your brain says, "Wait a second, that's exactly what I was looking for, and I know that because I've been thinking about that and making these affirmations." I know there are some nay-sayers about the whole affirmation thing. This is not the "you just say an affirmation and voila! It shows up." Although, I know in your case Cathy, and in many people's cases when you get really good at this and make it a part of your life, in fact, it sometimes appears that all you have to do is think about it and it shows up. Right?

KS: I gotta tell you this, I haven't had any money come through the ceiling yet and I have not won the lottery. (*laughs*) Neither one would be a bad thing to happen, but you know.

CG: Well I am waiting for you to do an affirmation for me so that the money will come through my ceiling.

KS: I'm still waiting!

CG: So every week we have a quote. This week, you actually mentioned this earlier although we did not talk about it beforehand… it is, "Passion and purpose go hand in hand. When you discover your purpose you will normally find that it is something that you are tremendously passionate about." That was written by Steve Pablina. He is a big time blogger. So what do you think about that?

KS: Wow, I love how things just have a way of connecting together! Oh my gosh, it's like magic.

CG: Would you agree with that statement?

KS: Absolutely. I would absolutely agree, yes.

CG: So what is your favorite quote or quotes? Do you have quotes that are posted on a bulletin board or maybe you share with others?

KS: I have several, as I think we all do. And sometimes it's like your kids, it's hard to pick your favorite. I'm going to share this one, "There are many things in life that will catch your eye, but only a few that will catch your heart. Pursue those."

CG: Love it!

KS: The thing about it is I do not know who said that. So! This would be kind of cool. If there is anyone out there that knows, contact us and let us know because I would love to know. I love that quote.

CG: Awesome. So if you could spread passion dust somewhere, and give passion for the day, what would you hope to accomplish?

KS: Is it sparkly?

CG: Of course!

KS: I think that if I could sprinkle passion dust I would put it all over the people who feel they're not good enough or they're not worthy and what they have doesn't mean anything. Everybody, every single person has value and worth and knowledge and so many great gifts to share. I would just sprinkle it all over those people so they would just feel loved and know that they have value and worth.

CG: I love that. That shows who you are, that you want to share that passion with others.

So, I'm not going to make you sing, but what song are you passionate about? Or what song gets you more passionate? We're not talking the TMI kinda stuff, but you know… Unless you want to Kathy! Then you go right ahead.

KS: (*laughs*)

CG: So what song are you passionate about? What song really epitomizes who you are?

KS: I just listened to this song this morning. A lot of people out there may not have ever heard of this gal, her name is Beckah Shae. She's got many songs, but she has one called *Life*. Just *Life*, and there are mornings that I just pull it up on YouTube and I just jump around and it gets me going and it gets me pumping and it's a fun song. I love all kinds of music by the way. Hard Rock and 50's and even a little Eminem or Pink. I just love all kinds of music. There may even be a few Justin Bieber songs that I like. (*laughs*)

CG: (*laughs*) All of Kathy Stovers secrets are now out!

KS: (*laughs*) I know… I know…

CG: It's your legacy that you are putting out there. You're hearing it here first, Kathy Stover likes Justin Bieber. There you go.

KS: It's just like… just one or two songs!

CG: Well I believe that music is the universal language. It speaks to those that otherwise might not hear and it really does get us going. Music can be what we put on when we are in a mood, maybe a solemn mood or a quite mood, we will put in a particular kind of music on. When we are in a "lets get up and go" in the morning… I already wrote down that name Beckah Shae down, I'm going to go check that out… Music motivates us and drives us and moves us hopefully in the direction that we need to go for that particular time and space.

Last question. What is your guilty passion?

KS: Guilty passion. Oh my goodness… well… I love, does it have to be something you eat?

CG: No, it can be anything, just keep it clean, we're on television.

KS: Okay, I love NASCAR. I love Harley Motorcycles. I LOVE chocolate. Love chocolate. Maybe not the good kind. I don't look at the label and see how many coordinates it's got or whatever makes it special. I just like it.

CG: So what people might not know about you and I, you and I actually bonded over our love for NASCAR and Harley's. How bizarre is that?

KS: Go figure! It's like I said, I go from mild mannered Kathy Stover, the social media strategist, and then I put on black leathers and I turn into Katrina the biker chick.

CG: Oh my gosh, I hope you take some pictures and you show that off on your social media.

KS: I will.

CG: Any last nuggets that you would like to share with our audience? Then I'll ask how they can get in touch with you. Of course I will let them know how they can get in touch with you via our tools, but is there anything you want to share with us?

KS: I think what I want to share is this. I want to share the fact that you, Caren Glasser, are such a beautiful-hearted woman. And for you to create a place and a space like this, for people to come and share their heart with others, and feel safe and comfortable is absolutely amazing and wonderful. Thank you so much for doing what you do. Not only with this, because you have a program to create books and an event planning business, and just a multitude of things that I can't even begin to list. So, when I think of passion, and I think of people, I think of you.

CG: Oh, thank you. That was unsolicited and thank you very much and it was ... wow... I just don't know what to say. Thank you. So how can people get in touch with you and find out how they can utilize your services, via either social media or internet TV... How can they get in touch with you?

KS: I am all over Facebook. A lot of me being in Facebook is through my clients, but I am in Facebook as well. So you can reach me through Facebook at /KathyStoverCA, the CA meaning California. I guess that it could also mean Canada, but I meant California. You can also Google me, and my website is KathyStover.com.

CG: Imagine that!

We are here to serve and support you. Kathy I want to thank you so much for being on with us today on *The Passion Point*. You rock, girlfriend!

KS: Thank you!

CG: So for all of you who have taken the time to spend with us today, we know that your time is valuable and we want to thank you for taking that time and sharing it with us. That goes also for those of you who are watching this afterwards, as we go into YouTube-land forever and ever and ever! We thank you for being with us. Bye! Bye!

HELEN BRAHMS
FEBRUARY 5, 2013

CG: Hello everyone, Caren Glasser here. I want to welcome you to this week's episode of *The Passion Point*. This is the show where we bring in different passionistas in our community and around the world that are following their passion and their purpose and actually making a living doing what they love. Today is no exception. I'm very excited to welcome our guest, Helen Brahms from HaveToCruise.com. She is the cruise coordinator extraordinaire! She is the woman that without her we would not be able to do our Passion Cruise that we do every year. She's really, really awesome. She's from New Zealand, you're going to notice that from her accent when she talks. You might not know she is from New Zealand, you might think she has a funny accent and I don't know where she's from!

HB: *(laughs)*

CG: But I'm letting you know, it's from New Zealand. We are really happy to have her here and I just want to give kudos to you, Helen, because we know that you are in the top ten of cruise planners in the world. How awesome is that? I'm not surprised to hear it because you really do bring so much value and service to the people that you serve. So, Helen, welcome to the show.

HB: Well thank you, Caren, it is a great honor and a privilege to be with you here this morning.

CG: I can't tell our listeners and our viewers how much I respect what you do. You are pretty amazing and you do it with such ease and grace. One would not know all the things that go on behind the scenes because you make it seem so easy. I would just like to tell our listeners that we did over 20 events last year and I was telling somebody the other day - I think you were standing there - there is a lot of stuff that goes into doing events. As an event producer, it's time consuming, it takes a lot of details, that's why I'm called "M" squared, Mama Minutia, its about all those details. But the reality is that the cruise that we do with you is probably the easiest thing that we do in terms of all of our events, which to the normal thinker does not make sense at all. We'll talk a little bit about that. We'll talk a little bit about you, right now.

Every week what we do is we start out with the definition of passion and this is what *Webster's* says, "Passion is an intense driving or overmastering feeling or conviction." So Helen, what is your definition of passion? How would you describe passion to our listeners?

HB: My definition of passion is finding something that you love to do and go out there and do it 110%. Just give it your all and even the little bumps along the way, they don't matter. There's a saying I heard one time, that if the dream is big enough, the facts don't count. That's how I see passion, is that if your passion is there and your drive is there to

18

do what you love to do, then the little bumps in the road? They don't matter. They don't count because you are doing what you love to do.

CG: I love that definition. Love that definition. So, what do you tell people that have kind of lost their way? They don't know what they are supposed to be doing and how they are supposed to be getting to wherever that dream is. How do you talk to people about following their passion?

HB: I just start with the basic question, of what do you love to do? And they could be selling houses, but that's not their real passion. Their real passion could be that they want to be out taking people around the city and be like a tour guide. And I go, "Why don't you? What's stopping you?"

It's like when people meet me and they find out I'm from New Zealand and they say, "I love New Zealand! It's such a beautiful country!" Oh! Great! When were you last there? "Oh, I've never been." And I'm like… okay… I'm thinking in my head, "How can you say you like my country and then say you've never been there?" I mean, if I haven't been somewhere I'll go, "That's a place I've always wanted to go, I love pictures of it." So I turn around and I say, "Well why haven't you been?" And then all the excuses start coming up. I just stand there and go, "So? So? So?" (*laughs*) Trying to basically get them talking themselves into a trip to New Zealand. It gets them thinking like, "I don't have the time." Well why not make the time?

CG: Right

HB: You know we all need to take a vacation, so why not make the time to go? So I just keep asking them questions and removing the excuses out of their way. So they have no excuses left. I found out that life is very short. We don't have time to make excuses, we've got to get out there and get it done.

19

CG: Oh my gosh, wise, wise words, Helen. Sometimes people just need to get out of their own way, get out of their own head and stop with the excuses. Manifest those intentions and put it down. If somebody wants to go to New Zealand, or if they think it's a wonderful country, why haven't they gone? Put it on their bucket list. Put it on their list of things they want to do and figure out how they're going to actually do what they're passionate about.

So. Tell us about your passion. What are you passionate about? I know, obviously cruising. Tell us how you came to this passion, how did you get into what you're doing?

HB: When I was little, in fact when I was growing up in New Zealand, we had a saying in New Zealand which was, "Don't leave home until you've seen the country." My parents literally took that to heart. They would "drag" us kids around the country during school holidays. We'd pack up the caravan, sorry, the campervan, and we would be off to a different part of New Zealand exploring. We would be there as a traveler and as a tourist, so we learned the definition between a traveler and a tourist as well. That ignited my love of travel.

Fast forward to five years ago when my husband was battling cancer, and we were in the most stressful time: we were off the charts stressed and my husband said, "We need to find a way to earn income from home." I was working part time and my husband wasn't working at all, and it was a lot of stress with all the chemo treatments that were going on and everything else. So we looked through the latest Entrepreneur Magazine that we had at the time and they had top 100 franchises. We are going through and saying, what about this? What about that? And then I said, "Oh! What about travel?" And my husband, whose parents had a travel agency, turned around and said, "You can't do travel from home!" I said, "There's a whole section here on home-based travel." So we looked into it and cruise planners was the number one franchise for the sixth year in a row. We delved into it, looked into it, researched into it and decided that's the one we wanted to go with. Once I got access to the cruise line so I could start doing the training programs, all of a sudden it was like BAM! (*snaps her fingers*) This is what I want to do!

From that point on it was how do I get out of my full time job and I was working in tourism at the time with the Marriott International. How do I leave my job at Marriott and get full time into this business? I just LOVED putting people on cruise ships. At that point, I hadn't even stepped foot on a cruise ship, I hadn't even taken a cruise! But I had found my passion and as they say, the rest is history.

CG: So, you just mentioned something. You were trying to figure out how to get out of your J-O-B , your Just Over Broke, Jump Out of Bed, right? And get into this enterprise and this new entrepreneurial world. So what were some of the steps that you did? Because I think this is really important, a lot of people that are in their jobs, their 9-5's, that are trying to find their passion and then they find it and they go, "Well how am I supposed to do this? I have a job!" What do you tell people? What did YOU do?

HB: My situation was a little unique. I was just working the cruise business part time, well really I was doing it full time hours because I was putting in the full 40 hours a week. When I wasn't at work, I was at home studying on the computer. We got the training done and all of that so then I thought, "How can I increase the business?" One of the things that I wasn't able to do at the time, because of my J-O-B, was that I wasn't able to get out there and network. I felt like that was holding me back, not being able to network.

What happened was that we were looking at moving from Virginia to California, and at the same time, the training department that I worked for at Marriott was undergoing a huge reshuffle. I applied for five jobs there and I will never forget this moment, it was June 16th of 2010 and it was my youngest stepson's 21st birthday, so a day to remember. We were

21

somewhere in the desert in California we had stopped and it was 103 degrees outside. We were slurping on ice cream and I got the call from the recruiting office at Marriot to say I did not get any of the five jobs I had applied for. I. Was. Ecstatic.

I said to her, "None of them?" And she said, "No, no." And I went, "That's AWESOME!" That was met with deathly silence. (*laughs*)

I was so excited because all of a sudden my biggest roadblock had been moved. I could get out there, I could get networking. I could start spreading the word, I was going into a new area, so it was a great time for me to have a clean slate. Let's get started, let's just move forward. So that's basically what happened. As soon as we got into town I started finding networking groups and everything else to join.

CG: Are you actually telling me that you walked out of your paying job and cold turkey just stepped into this? I mean you were obviously studying, and you were taking the programs and classes, but you just jumped in.

HB: Well at that point we had been doing the business part time for almost two years. So we did have some clients that we had built up but now I was able to go and escalate and get moving. By the end of that year I had more than doubled what I had done in the two years part time.

CG: So as a good friend of ours says all the time, Casey Eberhart, he says, "Opportunities multiply as there are seized." Would you agree?

HB: Absolutely! (*laughs*)

CG: This was an opportunity and I think our listeners and viewers can take this to heart. Sometimes, not just sometimes, I think all the times, you need to be listening, you need to be aware of the opportunities that come to you and cross your vision so that you know it is something that you want to do.

I often talk about manifesting your intentions. A lot of people will say, "Oh yeah, yeah. It's a bunch of hooey. What? You're just supposed to think it and it happens?" Well, no. But if you're not thinking it, how are you going to know when the opportunity comes to you? You need to have those thoughts in your head. Would you agree that that, in fact, is what happened with you? That you had those thoughts in your head and the opportunity arose?

HB: Absolutely. Don't get me wrong, I did enjoy my job with Marriot. I worked with some amazing people when I was there and I got to meet a lot of amazing people. But I felt like I was held back and I wasn't doing what my passion was. It wasn't until I got into my cruise planners business that I found what my passion was.

I have a huge love for customer service, so any job I've had since the age of 11, everything has been customer service orientated. But taking that customer service and helping people get on a cruise ship? I don't know who is more excited when my clients go on a cruise, my clients or me!

CG: Well, me! I was as excited as you! (*laughs*)

HB: I get ecstatic, especially when I'm in the office and I know I've got clients getting on the cruise ship. I'm just like, "Oh, yay! They are getting on the cruise ship!" I'm walking through in my mind, now they'll be at check-in, now they'll be doing this, they'll be doing that, they'll be going here, and dit, dah, dah, dah, dah! So thinking what they are going to be doing when they get back, it's like, "How was the cruise?"

CG: So what do you tell people, especially entrepreneurs and people that are working for themselves - following their passion - about "bright shiny objects."

23

HB: Oh they're just super fantastic and sparkly. (*laughs*)

CG: So for those of us, and entrepreneurs in general, when we see an idea, and you say, "Oh yes!" Sometimes it is a bright, shiny object and you have no business chasing it and sometimes it is a bright shiny object that you have every business and you should be chasing it. How do you discern when you are looking at opportunities that it's a good opportunity, or just a bright shiny object that's just taking your attention away from your path.

HB: Believe it or not, I get a gut feeling about it. Sometimes you have to dig to find that shiny object. It's like having the medal detector out and getting the little beep, beep, beep. Sometimes you know there's something beneath the surface, but you're not exactly sure so you dig and dig and dig. The gut tells you keep digging or the gut says walk away. So a lot of it is relying on my intuition and my gut feeling, you know, is this the right thing to be doing.

One thing I learned in my husband's cancer battle was, life is very short. You don't have time for the "I can'ts." Now I've got to turn the "I can'ts" into the "how can I's." You may not be able to do it exactly this way, but with a little alteration you can do it this way and off you go. Finding those bright shiny objects is just a matter of looking at the gut and saying, "Does this fit in with the plan?" And if it doesn't how can I turn it around so that it does or can I find somebody who can help that shiny object become even brighter.

CG: I love that, so let's kind of hone in on that right now. You look at bright, shiny objects as a good thing.

HB: Yes!

CG: Not necessarily an ADD moment, it's a good thing. It means that you look forward to these opportunities that arise and it's just a matter of discerning which one is going to work for you. And if you need help in chasing that bright, shiny object, or that next program or that next project , don't be afraid to find the help to take you to that next level. Correct?

HB: Correct and if it is not something that I should chase, it could still be a benefit for somebody else. So if it's a bright shiny object that I know would help somebody else with their business, I will say, "Hey, you need to go over here and you need to talk with this person."

CG: Awesome. You're a connector. There's no question that you are a connector because of what you do. You're a connector.

HB: I LOVE connecting people. (*laughs*)

CG: I love that about you. I resonate with that.

So each week we like to talk about the quote of the week. Today's quote is, "Purpose may point you in the right direction, but it's passion that propels you." That was written by Travis McAshan, he's an entrepreneur and web strategist. So what do you think about that quote? "Purpose may point you in the right direction, but its passion that propels you." Does that resonate with you?

HB: Absolutely. I love that one! Can you email me that? That might become my new favorite quote! (*laughs*)

CG: I definitely will email it to you. I love quotes, I put quotes up all the time, I love to have something that motivates me in the morning, that gets me up and I use it as part of my motivation to get through the day. What quote or quotes do you have in your back pocket that help motivate you?

25

HB: One of my most favorite people to listen to is Zig Ziglar and unfortunately he passed away not that long ago. One of my favorite quotes from him is, "If you can dream it, then you can achieve it. You'll get what you want in life if you help enough other people get what they want."

CG: Love that. Powerful. Would you not agree, Helen, that the world that we live in today, people that are successful and making a difference, it is because they are of service. So they are service first, right, and receiving second. Wouldn't you agree?

HB: Yes. Absolutely. One of the biggest things that I learned with networking is, it's not all about "me." It's about what I can do to help whoever it is I'm networking with. I'm always listening to the person, what is it that they do? What is it that they need? Who do I know that can help take them to the next level or help them with the situation that they currently have? So it's that connector thing in me coming out.

CG: And that makes you their go-to person, right?

HB: Yes.

CG: And so as you continue to help them fulfill their needs, when they are out there and they hear about somebody who is looking to do an event or do something a little different, then eventually, if you are working with them closely, they will refer to you as well. The whole referral marketing and the whole networking industry, no matter what networking group that you might belong to, has a "serve first" mentality.

HB: Correct, yes.

CG: So, Helen, if could spread passion dust somewhere and give passion for the day, what would you hope to accomplish?

26

HB: Oooh! I would have a lot of people on a cruise ship networking. (*laughs*) So they can connect. Why not do it on a cruise ship? I mean, I want to say it's a confined space, but cruise ships are big, you're not enclosed, as you guys found out in the Promote Your Passion cruise last year. But if I could put people on a cruise ship that could all help each other, and let them go sailing for seven days, let them get to know each other, like we did with the Passion Cruise, that would be what I'd like. Put the people on cruise ships and let them just network and find other people who can share their passion and help them with some struggle they're having in business.

That's why I absolutely love what you are doing with the Promote Your Passion cruise, that's exactly what you do. You bring on people that can serve the people's interests in what they are doing with their business and things, and at the same time they are networking and they are learning. But also you get back, the speaker's get back what they give out. What you give out, you get back tenfold. It works beautifully. So that would be my thing. Hit the docks, everybody go on a cruise and have a blast.

CG: So we can make your wishes come true. We have another cruise coming up at the end of this year, our next annual cruise. Just as a little side note. Those of you who are listening and want to find out how you can come on the next Promote Your Passion cruise that Helen Brahms is coordinating, we have some amazing speakers and break-out sessions and keynote speakers. It's a really great opportunity to learn, to network, to kick your 2014, the next year, into high gear. We're going to discuss later how to find out more about Helen and how she can help you booking your cruises and also how you can participate and come on the next cruise.

What was wild about that cruise is that we started with a respectable amount of people. Not a whole lot of people but enough that it was a really, really fabulous cruise, the first one, and from that cruise we actually doubled the amount of rooms for next year already, even before we got out the gate. So that's kudos to you Helen, you do such an amazing job and you make people feel so comfortable. If you are an event producer or an event planner out there and you're watching this, I strongly suggest that you get in touch with Helen to talk about how to do your events on a cruise ship. We're not going to get into any details about that, you're going to want to connect with her. But really, this is the wave of the future. This is really a great way, an affordable way (believe it or not) to produce your events. I've actually gone to doing my events only this way, to be honest because it makes sense. She takes away all of the stress. So I just wanted to give you a real big pat on the back for that because you made my life incredibly easy and I just adore working with you.

Okay! So what song are you passionate about?

HB: Oh, there are so many songs out there, Caren! (*laughs*) When you first told me I had to think about a song I was like "Oh, jeepers, what songs do I have."

Anything that's upbeat. I'm *Walking on Sunshine* is one of my favorites. I actually have that on my ipod for when I go to the gym and doing my cardio, I have about two hours of songs lined up there. I listen to them while I'm doing my cardio as well as the weight-training portion of my workout. *Walking on Sunshine* is definitely one that I enjoy.

CG: I was expecting you to say *Supercalifragilisticexpialidocious* because you are super fantastic and sparkling. I thought that might be a song that was in your wheelhouse.

HB: No, *Walking on Sunshine* would be one of my favorites. It's just the beat of the song! You just want to get out there and you just want to go, "WOO!"

CG: I love that song, it's a great song.

28

HB: *Celebration* is one that I like, because I like to celebrate life. Anything that's got a good, upbeat tune to it that has a good positive message on it, that's what I love.

CG: Get your juices flowing. So obviously Helen is telling us to get that music that motivates us to take that next step and get going.

HB: (*starts dancing in her seat*)

CG: There she is! She's dancing over there!

HB: (*laughs*)

CG: We should turn some music on! (*laughs*)

So our last passion question. What is your guilty passion?

HB: Chocolate. (*laughs*) If it's got chocolate in it, I'm there.

CG: Oh my gosh, I hear you on that.

Any last minute things you would like to share with our listening and viewing audience about you? Maybe a message that people can take to heart and pursue their passion?

HB: Life is too short to let things get in the way. The cancer journey we were on, we met a lot of people. Out of my caregivers group, I'm the only one with my spouse still with us. That showed just how short life is. When you've seen fathers leaving behind young children, we were seeing families be torn apart by cancer. It really drove home the fact that life is short. People still just go, "Oh that's you, that's your children." Trust me. Nobody wants to be on that journey. Nobody wants to go through anything like that. I don't want to live life with regrets. I don't want anybody else to live life with regrets. I want to be one of those people that when the time comes to meet or pass through to whatever is on the other side (whatever your beliefs are), I want to be the one who slides in at the end and says, "Wow! What a ride!" I want other people to have that kind of feeling too.

Life is to be lived. Take that passion, run with it, don't bury it deep down inside because then you're going to have a life full of regrets. Life is too short to be living that way. Find what your passion is, get out there, live it to the fullest, and remember, don't say, "I can't," say, "How can I."

CG: You are inspirational. Thank you. So if our listeners want to get in touch with you, I know that you have on your screen a website and your phone number, but why don't you tell everyone how they can get in touch with you? So where do they go?

HB: They will go to my website, which is HaveToCruise.com or call 818-528-8300.

CG: Awesome. Helen, thank you so much for joining us today on *The Passion Point*. You are an inspiration, your story is an inspiration. I know that anyone listening to you and what you have accomplished, in really quite a short amount of time, is amazed. You are an amazing woman and I am honored and blessed to call you my friend.

Again, I want to thank everyone for being on with us today. You have plenty of choices for how you spend your time. It's valuable and we want to thank you for spending your time with us, Helen and myself on *The Passion Point*. We hope that you will join us again next week when we visit with you on next week's episode of *The Passion Point*. Helen, thank you so much for being with us.

HB: Thank you, Caren. It's been an honor and a pleasure to be here.

CG: Goodbye everyone, see you next week.

STACEY HALL

APRIL 16, 2013

CG: Hello everyone, Caren Glasser here; Promote Your Passion. I want to welcome you to this week's episode of *The Passion Point*. We are so excited to have our guest today with us, Stacey Hall. I want to introduce Stacey to everyone, give you a little bio, a little introduction. I'm going to read from something right now and then we're going to bring Stacey right into the show.

Stacey Hall is the founder of the whole institute of intuitive wellness, saving the lives of people stressed to the snapping point. Does that sound like you? I know it sounded like me. I had an amazing conversation with Stacey just a week ago and oh my gosh, what she was able to do with me in just one hour was frickin' awesome.

Having reached a point of complete physical, emotional, and mental depletion in 2005, Stacey Hall declared, "I want to learn how to heal my heart and then help others to heal their hearts." So her message, be energized, be powerful, and keep your eye on your be-all has become the rally call for the worldwide Chi-To-Be movement that is uplifting the globe with commitment, harmony and inspiration, one person at a time. She's also the author of *Chi-To-Be, Achieving Your Ultimate B-All* and creator of the Chi-To-Be master program. She's the author of the global bestseller, *Attracting Perfect Customers, the Power of Strategic Synchronicity* which has been translated into numerous languages since its publication in 2001. I'm excited because we have Stacey with us on *The Passion Point* today. So welcome Stacey to *The Passion Point*, come on in!

SH: It is such a joy, a true part of my passion to be with you, Caren. Thank you so very much for inviting me.

CG: Well, I'm really excited because we had an actual face-to-face meeting just a week ago, which is always fun because we live in this social media world. When we live in the online world, so many times our connections and the people that we get to know, we never meet in person. We end up meeting them just online and it almost feels like we know them but when you finally have that offline connection, would you not agree, it changes everything.

SH: Absolutely, Caren. We're friends now, not just acquaintances.

CG: Absolutely, and it's funny when you look on social media, you can "friend" people and that's sort of silly when you realize when you get offline, that's where the friendships really happen. I'm not saying that you can't create community and networking friendships online, but taking it offline? That's where the magic happens, so I just want to thank you so much for being with us today.

SH: My joy.

CG: So every week we start our show with *Webster's* definition of passion. I always like to hear what my guests think of that definition, and then

34

have you tell me your definition of passion. *Webster's Dictionary* says, "Passion is an intense driving or overmastering feeling or conviction." Would you agree?

SH: I do actually agree. I think it also has the power of intention with it.

CG: Very, very nice. So do you live your life with intention?

SH: I would like to say that I do everything I possibly can to live my life with intention and with passion for, as you mentioned, my Be-All. I'm going to say today, and you can hear there's a little bit of a froggy in my throat. I want to address that right away. I am passionate about cleansing my body and getting very well. I'm sure you're going to ask me about my background here in a moment, so I just want to say thank you everyone for your patience with me today. I'm going through another stage of my detoxification program but it seems to have lodged in my throat today. (*laughs*)

But yes! Everything I do… let's put it this way. If there is no intention to it, then why do it? If I'm not clear what I want to get out of the energy I'm investing, then why do it? That would be what I encourage everyone to consider because often people are doing for other people and they say, "I had to do this" or "I have to do that." We don't have to do anything once we are over the age of 18! At least here in the United States we don't. So if we are doing something for someone else, then there must be an intention behind it. Not a "have-to" unless someone literally has a gun against our head.

CG: I really like that. I actually think that's a great quote, "If there's no intention to it, why do it?" That should be one of the quotes that you put your name to. I love that.

SH: (*laughs*) I appreciate it.

CG: It would be great with a photo and that quote and your name. I would buy it.

SH: Thanks, Caren.

CG: So that's a little bit of a view on your passion, and that's just great at explanation and I think it says so much. I've heard your story, I've heard part of your story and I would love for you to share with us how you came to be doing what you're doing - today helping people alleviate stress and find balance in their lives. Tell us about where you've come from.

SH: Where I came from was a bestselling first book. That might seem a little bragging, if you will, but it's actually not. It was a very humbling experience for me because it was through a success that I had dreamed and envisioned. It came as a result of the very thing I wrote about, my book that I co-authored called *Attracting Perfect Customers, the Power of Strategic Synchronicity,* I actually attracted an abundance of people to be of service to. However, I was of the mind that I had to sacrifice my life for others.

I had put myself out there to be of service, so that meant with every waking breath, every drop of energy I had, I was supposed to be helping others. I ran myself into the ground in a variety of ways. Physically, by not taking good enough care. Emotionally, by fighting against the emotions of, "I need to take care of myself but I can't, I have to take care of other people." Mentally, feeling like everyday I was slipping further and further away and not doing what it took to rejuvenate.

And being run by fear. That's really what it was. Fear, took my life. And I would say the only reason I didn't actually die is because there was enough love within me for others and myself that I was willing to stop myself before it got that to that point.

36

But what did happen is, I wound up with adrenal failure for two years and three months. I know exactly the day my body said, "no more." It was January 28th, 2005. Because I finally did have the chance to rest. I had resigned from my ownership of my first company to start taking care of myself. My body realized I was serious and said, "Okay, well then, we're collapsing now," which happened about three weeks afterwards.

I also know that day that I really started to feel much better. It was in March, we'll say mid-March, of 2007. Because that was the day I was introduced to essential oils and the power of regenerating our own energy. And they really had a profound effect on me. With that, I was able to start getting out of bed, start eating right again, start taking nutritional supplements and start looking at what it was that I did. The choices I had made. What intentions did I have that did not deliver on the result.

I started making different choices. Information came through to me very quickly and I call that information my energy surges. Because that's exactly what they did, they helped me surge my energy back to a place where I was healthy and well again. Now, it took years to get me to that point, so it's taking me years to recover completely. As they say, you peel back the layers of the onion, one peel at a time. So I'm still in the process of discovery and learning and cleaning and clearing, all of which is with a real intention now to achieve three elements towards my life's goals.

One of those is to be a number one *New York Times* Best-Selling Author. I'm a best-selling author on Amazon, I want to get to the top of *New York Times*. Because that means I was able to share these energy surges with thousands of people because everyone right now I think is stressed to the snapping point. I really do believe on some level.

CG: I do, and you know what Stacey? As I listen to you, I am sure that people are also listening to you saying, "I resonate with that." I resemble you. I know I had the same feeling when I spoke with you, your story is so powerful. I'm going to let you continue because I just wanted to interject.

SH: And I'm going to say that the only reason it was worth it, to go through what I did, is that one of my worst days when I was still in bed and I didn't think that I was ever going to get out, I really just laid it out to God and said, "If you will show me how to get better, I promise you I will pay attention to everything you show me, everything that works, and I will share it with other people." So to be able to be here with you on *The Passion Point*, Caren, is the fulfillment of that intention. I love it. That's why I said it IS my joy.

It is a complete, fabulous experience to share with others, that within each of us, we have everything we need to regenerate ourselves. Most people don't realize that! When we were sick as kids, we turned to others. We turned to our parents or we turned to other adults. Very few people had to rely on themselves as children to figure out how to get better.

So it's very common, there's no reason for anybody to feel bad that they don't know how to take care of themselves. But once we're adults and we're out on our own, it's important that we know that within us we have everything we require physically, emotionally, mentally and spiritually. Here's a little exercise that I'm going to do for everyone. To prove it.

To do this, we sit quietly, and we put our feet flat on the floor. We are going to cross arms and our hands. We let the crown of our head raise up to the sky, and we take a few deep breaths to center ourselves. We can do this with closed eyes or opened eyes, either one. We can say to ourselves, "Okay. Physical body, on a scale of one to 10. How energized am I feeling right now in my physical body?" And Caren? You can do this, I won't call you out on it, but you just go ahead and do it for yourself, I'm doing it for myself.

Clearly, I wouldn't say I'm a ten in my physical body because I have some issues going on. I can say that I am about an eight, because I'm not sick, I know I'm releasing. And then I would say, "Okay, physical body, what do you need in order to get to a 10?" And I wait and I listen. My body is saying, "Well, you know, you woke up in middle of the night and you could have used an extra couple hours of sleep, so you can do that. Some more water, when the show is over would be good, Stacey. And taking it a little easier today," that's what my physical body needs. And I say, "Good." That will get me up to a ten.

Now I'm going to go to my emotional body. So in my emotions, on a scale of one to 10, where am I? Now I can honestly tell you where it is as I'm sitting here, my emotions are on neutral, which means I'm a ten. I'm not being tugged in any one particular way. A little earlier, when we were having some technical difficulties, I had some apprehension, and a little disappointment, so I would have said back then my emotional body would have been around a seven during that time. Right now with everything going well, feeling great, sharing what I want to share, I'm a ten, so nothing more to do there right now.

Mental body, scale of one to ten, I'm feeling really clearheaded. I'm going to say a nine and a half. So then I'm going to say, mental body, what do you need to get to that full ten? I'm hearing water and a little bit of food. A little extra food. That will get ya to a ten.

And then spiritual body, which some people might interpret to be your religious body. That's not what I mean I just mean in my spirit, the place where when it is a 10, I am completely calm. What's my number? So spirit body, scale of one to 10, how am I doing? And I'm saying I'm a 10. I'm feeling calm. I'm with a good friend, having a great chat, I'm a 10. Nothing more to do there.

So I come away from that experience with exactly what to do to energize myself. And that's just one of 11 energy surges I share in my book. And when I say that's one, that's the chi-generating rituals and yet I give many other kinds of chi-generating rituals, in the book. It didn't cost anything to do that, did it?

CG: No, and I think it's awesome and I think it's a great exercise. Would you suggest people do this when they wake up in the morning or at any time during the day, or at the end of the day? Is this the ritual that you do?

SH: Yes and yes and yes and yes! Yes, as soon as we wake up. Now I'll tell you, my morning ritual, soon as my eyes open. The very first thing I say is, "I am an attraction master. I am attracting to me all that supports me in achieving my B-all goals." And then I'll check in with my chakras and I'll make sure they are activated. I'll go through my root chakra red, my sacral chakra orange, solar plexus chakra yellow, heart chakra green, throat chakra blue, third eye chakra indigo, ground chakra violet, and star chakra white. Just to make sure all those chakra energies are open and live. Then I'll say my B-all to myself.

Now I'm ready to get out of bed and start the day. As I start to get out of bed, if I'm not feeling 100%, like you could imagine this morning, not 100%, then I check in with the four bodies. If during the day I start to feel my energy wane, and we all know when our energy is waning, I'll do this very quick, very simple exercise. It takes less than a minute to figure out what I'm meant to do next. And that was what I did not do all those years. I did not check in. I just kept pushing.

CG: So for those who are listening, I know at the end of our conversation today, we're going to be sending them to connect with you. I know that this information is in your book, as well as they may just want to connect with you and have a quick call to see how you might be able to work with each other. To help people get out of that place, that space that they're in. What do you tell people that are stumbling around out there and they can't seem to find their passion, they can't seem to figure out what their passion is? What do you tell people?

40

SH: I have a very simple exercise for people because I hear this all the time. And Caren, thank you for sharing, we will talk about how people can boost their energy very quickly more after the show. For people who don't know what their passion is or don't feel passionate, this is what I say. Of course, my terminology is the "B-All" as in the be-all, end-all goal. People say to me, well I don't have one. And I'll say to them, "Then why are you still here on earth? What are you doing?"

CG: That's a high five for you.

SH: Yeah. Right there back at ya! Truly! Why are you still choosing to be alive? And they might say to me, "Because I would never consider killing myself," and I say, why? Well because there's gotta be something for me to do here. So you're B-all is being of service. To be helpful in whatever way you can. And they'll say, "Oh! Yes!" Okay great, that's your B-all. Or they might say because my children depend upon me. See, so it's really important to you to take good care of your children. "Yes." Well isn't that you passion? Isn't that your B-all? "Oh! I thought it was supposed to be some big, momentous kind of thing!" No.

CG: Don't you find that some people think it's has to be this big thing when really in fact it's inside. Just listening to what's inside.

SH: Right. And what they are doing to themselves, as what I always say is, they're "shoulding" on themselves. They're thinking that they should have something bigger and better instead of, "this is big and best for me."

CG: Right. So I'm one who likes to live by quotes. I love a quote in the morning. For me, that's something that gets me going in the morning. I'm always posting quotes whether it's on social media, and my email signature has a quote in it. I mean, it's just something to work towards and just start your day with. So today's quote, that I've already posted on Facebook, interestingly enough, and already people are posting on that post! It obviously resonated, and I picked this one because of you, and it's, "The best part of life is not just surviving, but thriving, with passion, style, compassion, generosity, humor, and kindness."

SH: Yes, I absolutely agree.

CG: I thought you'd like that one. What quotes do you resonate with? You just made one earlier, so that was one that I think you should just use.

SH: I will, I will absolutely. I was going to say, my intention was to create magic with you today so that was one! As soon as we are off I'm going to go ahead and tweet it and post it. Here's one of my quotes. My best quotes come out of my conversations with my clients because I allow myself to be in their space. Magic happens between us. So one that came out of my mouth that I went, 'Woah, that's pretty good,' is, "Instead of shoulding on ourselves, lets choose for ourselves."

CG: Love that.

SH: And you reminded me of that when the "shoulding" came up. Yes, instead of "shoulding" on ourselves, lets choose, and you can say lets choose powerfully, for ourselves.

CG: I like that. I like that. So that's great and… what do you think about the power of quotes? I just told you I like them, but what do you think about quotes? Do you think that they do a service for people, or a disservice for people? Do we rely too much on them?

SH: I can't imagine. If a quote is uplifting, how could it possibly do a disservice? If it makes us feel better, if it gives us a boost in our energy, then it's all good. Especially if quotes make us laugh a little because laughter is so wonderful. I make it a point: I do share quotes. I also like to retweet when I'm on Twitter. I like to honor somebody who offers a fabulous quote like you do, by retweeting for them and spreading it through the world. It's very important to me, so I do this every day.

The other kinds of quotes that I enjoy and I am known for (as are all the "Chi-Lifters" who are participating in Chi-To-Be) are "I am" quotes. You know, the I AM with the capital A, capital M. Because, as it says, anything that goes after that determines our reality. And We Speak, I'm using the huge We, and there were times when I was part of that We. But most people speak to themselves in a way they would never let anyone else ever speak to them. So another part of my morning ritual is to speak "I AM" statements to myself that are who I intend to be.

So today, there was a major incident in the world, probably a few of them, but one right here in the United States. My quote for myself today was "I am focused, on the good in the world, and all around me to remind myself that no matter what else might come into me about the incident, there is still good in the world and there's lots of it." So that's how I lift myself up with an "I AM" quote.

CG: I love I AM statements as well. What I do is actually send myself a greeting card, a card that I write in "I am" intentions, quarterly that I mail to myself and it comes as a surprise and I open it up and I put it on my bulletin board. They are definitely "I am." Our mind thinks in the present not in the future or in the past. When you say I am, we are actually experiencing and our mind is experiencing in the present. So when you say I am a successful entrepreneur, or I am a highly successful, highly sought after, what ever it is, your mind internalizes it as right now and today. I Am is so important and thank you so much for bring that up for those who are watching, today and in the future. As you know, we stream this, this is on YouTube and will go out forever and ever. For people that are watching this, the power of "I am" statements can change your life quite frankly.

SH: I know they have for me. I know they have for many of the people I am coaching and have coached. I say "have coached" because that is the whole idea of a coach, right? The idea is to eventually eliminate the need for a coach because we got all of the tools to be able to go on. I Am statements have become one of the most effective, fastest tools. I am all about velocity and ease to boost our energy. Right there. Just saying, "I am."

And if we can't believe it, here's another tip, I would say there's a real possibility that "I am." There's a real possibility that "I am." I have met people who say I just can't feel it in my body, it feels like I'm lying. Okay, but if you say, "there's a real possibility that I am," the mind will accept that there's a possibility that it is true.

CG: And somebody that I know, Linda Jones, and I'm going to contribute this to her, she taught me this. One of the techniques that she does in her "I Am" statements is in between the "I am" that might not be believable right this second, she puts a real statement. So, you might say "I am creating mass income now." And then you would say, "I am Caren Glasser." Your mind says, oh yeah, that's true. You are Caren Glasser, maybe the other statement must be true too." So she literally puts a real statement that's completely real. I live here, or I do this, so that your brain is almost tricked into believing, even the ones that you don't believe yet.

SH: I love that! I'm going to contribute that to Linda Jones as well. I am going to continue to add that onto the coaching that I do, with her blessing.

CG: Yeah! It's really powerful and when she shared that with me, and she shared with a couple of people, it really makes a difference. Your brain is like, "Oh, that is me! Oh! Yeah!" You're tricking your brain basically.

SH: Yes, oh how fabulous.

CG: Isn't that kind of cool?

SH: It's not even kind of cool. It's great!

CG: (*laughs*) It's fun to share stuff like that. So now I have a fun question. And that is: If you could spread passion anywhere around the world, onto anyone around the world, who would you spread it on, and what would you hope to accomplish?

SH: I'm going to take a moment to really think because I could give you a really fast response. (*pause*) I'm going to take that question into my heart for a moment. (*pause*) So the most important thing in the world to me is to make God smile everyday. That's truly. If the powers-that-be came to me and said, I could not do that ever again. That I would have to lay in bed until my body atrophied, because I would be too worried about getting out of bed and doing something that would harm my health. So I'm going to answer the question this week here, I do my best to do that everyday and I do it according to how I am guided. So I wouldn't change anything, about the way that I'm living my life right now. That's the answer to it. That's is my mission in life, to support people connecting with their passions, connecting with their B-all, so they can live and help others do it, so for me it happens one person at a time.

CG: Thank you. One person at a time, I like that.

So do you have a song that you are passionate about? A song that helps you get into the space of moving, working, creating, finding passion. What is that song?

SH: Okay. Can I have three, please?

CG: You can have as many as you want.

SH: Alright. The first is, and this is absolutely a shameless plug, there's actually a Chi-To-Be theme song that was created by Joey Malotti. Joey happens to be a member of Barry Manilow's band and he produced the Chi-To-Be audio series. In the recording sessions he was moved to create a Chi-To-Be theme song and people go to my website at Chi-To-Be.com you will be able to hear it. When it comes on, turn your speakers up!

So that's one.

CG: Can somebody purchase it?

SH: Yes, it's purchasable. Absolutely and we give the information there on how to do that. In addition, there is *Don't Stop Thinking About Tomorrow* by Fleetwood Mac

CG: Love that.

SH: And *Better Days* which is on the soundtrack of *eat, pray, love*. And the name of the artist just went out of my head, [*Editor's Note: Eddie Vedder*] but if the Chi-To-Be theme song had not come through the way it did, I probably would have contacted the artist to see if I could use *Better Days* as the theme song for Chi-To-Be. It just moves me to tears in a very happy way.

CG: I'm going to check that out. I really liked the book but I never saw the movie. We're doing a playlist, by the way, of songs that resonate with all of our guests. We are going to do a whole playlist that will be available for people to, you know, get their juices flowing.

SH: I love this!

CG: Okay, so, one last question. What is your guilty passion? Do you have a guilty passion that you're going to share with the public now, that won't be private anymore?

SH: Yes! Well, let me put it this way. I do my best to not feel guilty about it, but I'm a chocolate lover. I absolutely am a chocolate lover. The richer, the darker, the better. I used to have a lot of guilt surrounding it because it was excessive, and as part of my detoxing and my cleansing process, it has become far less excessive. So now I only eat it when I really can enjoy it. I don't use it for dealing with emotions anymore. So! Not so guilty, but that is absolutely my pleasure along with, and this I'm not guilty about at all, I take an essential oil infused bath almost every morning. Those two things. Sometimes I can combine them together and that is absolutely heaven for me!

CG: Heaven! Heaven, heaven, heaven! (*laughs*) Well you've mentioned essential oils and we've run out of time, but I want people to know that you are a veritable wealth of all things that make somebody really feel at peace and bring a sense of calm. One of the things you use is essential oils and the healing aromatherapy and things like that. We didn't really have a chance to touch on that but when people reach out, I'm going to ask them to remember to ask you about it. It's something so important and I just started getting involved in that for myself as well. I want to make sure that people ask you about that. So as we said, there's a lot of ways you can get in touch with Stacey. You could go to her website, Stacey, give us your website again?

SH: It is Chi-To-Be.com. If you put a /blog after that you get a free subscription to my chi-lifting blog. Also, if you just go to Chi-To-Be.com you'll see my passions which are Chi-To-Be and everything Chi-To-Be, aromatherapy and also the Nia technique which is a fabulous form of movement that is done all around the world. It's a wonderful way of keeping our energy high as well. It's for people who don't like to exercise, and feel that they want to exercise.

CG: Awesome. Well I want to thank you Stacey, so much for being with me. And we didn't even… there's so much we could talk about that we could have just gone on for hours but unfortunately we only have half an hour on this particular show. So I want to invite you to come back and join us again.

SH: Anytime! And Caren, I'm thinking about making you a regular on the Chi-To-Be experience radio show too. Because as we talked about, our messages are so similar they belong together.

CG: Absolutely. So I just want to thank you for taking time out of your day and just sharing with us just a little piece of you so that all of our viewers and our listeners and networks out there have a chance to experience, Stacey Hall. Because you're awesome.

SH: Aw Caren, thank you. You know they say it takes one to know one and in this case, I know that is true!

CG: (*laughs*) Well thank you and I want to thank our listeners because we know that you have choices every single day how to spend your time and we want to thank you for spending time with us today. We do this show every single week, so please come back and join us again. If you'd like to get in touch with Stacey, go to the Chi-To-Be website. Thank you so much and have a great day everyone and we will see you all next week.

DIANE CONKLIN
APRIL 30, 2013

CG: Hello everyone, Caren Glassner here and welcome to this week's episode of *The Passion Point*. Each week we bring you passionistas from around the world who are following their passion and making a living doing what they love.

Today I am really excited to have my good friend Diane Conklin joining us. She is an internationally known author, entrepreneur, coach, consultant, event planner, speaker, copywriter, philanthropist, yadda, yadda, yadda… Oh my God! I'm exhausted just saying all those things but it's all true! You really have gotten your message out there and made a mark. It's one of the reasons I'm really excited that we're friends. As you know our story goes back to when I was just getting into the industry that I'm in. I was looking to see, "Who do I want to be just like?" and it was you Diane. And here we are friends. So welcome, Diane, to *The Passion Point*.

DC: Well thank you, Caren. That is a great compliment. I'm happy to be here and honored to call you a friend. So thank you very much, I appreciate it.

CG: So today we're going to talk about you. It's all about you. We're going to talk about your passion.

DC: I love that!

CG: I've been following you and I want to get to the heart of who Diane Conklin is. We are going to start our show by giving the *Webster's Dictionary* definition of what "passion" is. They say that passion is an intense, driving or over-mastering feeling and conviction. That's what *Webster's* says. What do you say passion is?

DC: Passion is all about your heart. Passion is all about, "What is the thing that you would do all day, every day, that fuels you." What gives you more energy and you wouldn't even care if no one ever paid you a penny. It's that thing that you feel so strongly about in your life that you could almost substitute the word "purpose" for passion. It's the thing that you are here to do.

It's not necessarily just one thing. We have multiple things that we are passionate about in our lives. Our businesses may be different, but I think the passion thing for me ... you just said that you want to know who Diane Conklin really is, that's a heart thing, not a head thing.

CG: I love that answer. It is totally on point. In fact, Promote Your Passion talks about finding your passion and turning that into your purpose so that you can create that life that you desire. So I totally agree with you.

50

So, tell us how Diane Conklin got to where she is today. I know that your journey has taken you across state lines. It has taken you all over the place. Tell us your journey and tell us what your passion is.

DC: I think the journey starts back as early as being that kid on the farm. I grew up on a 75 acre farm in Ohio and even back then I knew there was something calling me. There was something bigger for me... nothing wrong with where I grew up, for anyone who knows me... but there was always this tugging feeling that there was something more for me. So for me it's been about a journey of discovery. It's been a journey about being okay with finding who I am and then living that. Of not being afraid of that and not being ashamed of saying "I grew up on a farm and I'm a country girl at heart." You can take the girl out of the country but not the country out of the girl. Living that, just being who you are and knowing the right people are going to be attracted to that, I think is sort of the big thing.

So for me, my passion has been the same my whole life. It's about helping people. A lot of people say this so I want to qualify this. I have a masters degree in exercise physiology. That degree was about helping people on the level of changing their fitness, changing their health, changing their lives. Somehow, though that was fulfilling as marketing and fulfilling on the business side, somehow that was never quite enough for me. The thing that charges me now, the passion that I have now, helping people in their businesses, allows me to really use what I call the RIPPLE Effect. The acronym that I use for that is Repetition In Place Produces Little Effects Somewhere. I'll repeat that.

CG: I'm writing.

DC: Repetition In Place Produces Little Effects Somewhere. So when you think about that pebble that I get to drop in the water... today I'm talking to you, but in effect I'm talking to a lot of people because this is aired, people will see it later... So the ripple effect today is not just with Caren, it's with all the people who are listening to this.

CG: Right.

DC: The great thing is that if I say something today that inspires somebody, and makes a difference in their life, with that one, then they go out and tell it to ten. Those ten tell it to three or four. My effect then doesn't just effect you or just effect them. It has the potential to effect thousands and possibly hundreds of thousands. That's the thing that excites me. That's the reason I get up in the morning.

I have a note here that I just got yesterday from a guy that I coached and worked with. Then I did something with him; the two of us co-ventured a project. He sent me this great note thanking me. It literally says, "You're a hero to me and I love you." That's why I do what I do. I have that stuff in my office because we all have those days when it's not that fun. When I look at that I say to myself, "That's what it's about for me. That's why I do what I do." So there's a long answer to a short question.

CG: No, it's a great answer. Let's delve even deeper. Tell us what you do. How do you help businesses?

DC: Complete Marketing Systems is the name of my company. Essentially what we do is exactly that. We help companies through marketing, social media, direct response, event planning, and my big specialty is information marketing. We help small businesses and entrepreneurs to grow their businesses. We do that through marketing strategy. We do that through business techniques. We do that through a lot of different media. It's what I call integrating their marketing and their businesses so that they can reach six and seven figures in their business. To have more fun! To take more time off and enjoy their lives! Essentially what I do is teach people how to go from owning a job to owning a business.

CG: What do you tell people who are stumbling around out there? They have a passion and they have decided to go out and make a living doing what they love. They get out there and go, "Uhhhh… now what? What do I do first? What do I do second?" How do you help guide them on the right path?

DC: I think the biggest thing is that you have to have a plan. Some of my clients love my acronyms, some of them don't. (*laughs*) But the whole thing is that you can't go out sort of willy-nilly and just say I'm going to do this thing. I have this passion and I want to just go make money at it. It may or may not be viable. I hate to be the bearer of bad news but it may or may not be viable.

If I weigh a 100 lbs and I'm a guy, and I want to go out and be an MMA fighter, well, I'm not really sure that is going to work for you and be successful. So are there ways you can tweak that? Are there ways you can take that passion and that love and change it? Maybe you could be a trainer. Maybe you can be that guy that sits and commentates. There are a lot of different things you can do with that passion. It doesn't have to be that you are a fighter.

I base everything I teach on another acronym, PLANS. Plan and Prepare, Leverage, Action, Next and Now, and Strategies and Systems. I don't care where you are in your business, where you are in your life even. If you look at that acronym you can grow your business or start your business from there and if you do those things and you implement, it's going to grow.

CG: That's really, really important and I want to go back to what you just said about having a passion but it may not makes sense. That is exactly what you do. I would even take it one step further. You need to make sure your passion is something that is going to sell, period. You may be passionate about knitting, but that may not be the way you are going to make your living. There may not be enough people out there in that niche that are going to want to buy that. So how do people figure out if their pastime is something that is actually monetizable?

DC: That's a great question, Caren. I'm glad we came back to that point. The first thing I would tell you is go see if other people are selling things in that niche. Whatever the area is, go do a Google search on it. If there are other things available, don't let that scare you. Be excited about that. Because if there are already other things already on the market, then more than likely, there's a little more research to do, that there is a market. If you don't come up with anything when you do a Google search, you don't want to be a pioneer, because you know how they all ended up, right?

CG: (*laughs*) Absolutely, I totally know how they ended up.

DC: Laying in the back 40 with arrows in their backs! Don't blaze a new trail. If you are the only person it probably means there isn't a market. Do your research. You can find all the magazines, all the publications, all the newsletters and all the associations that associate with the thing you have an interest in. See what the population is. Are there people out there buying things already in that area. If there are, delve in and go for it. Do a survey of people. We tend to do things, and have passions in areas that we are already involved in. So ask around. Ask your friends, "Hey, would you invest in this? Is this a good idea? Would you want this?" And then go from there.

CG: I think that what you just said is so important. I assume that you are somebody that looks at keyword research, right?

DC: Absolutely.

CG: So for those of you out there that are going, "Keyword research? What does that mean?" That is just a way of going into Google and searching for phrases and figuring out what people are actually looking

54

for. And thank you so much for telling people not to get frightened by the fact that other people are looking for what you want to do. In fact that just gives you the lightbulb that says, "Ah! People like this!"

DC: Exactly, you have a market.

CG: Exactly!

So I love quotes. I wouldn't say I live my life by quotes, but everyday I try to find something that's going to motivate me and get me going for the day. Today I found a quote by Oprah Winfrey, which is really interesting because it ties in right to what you were talking about and I can say we did not talk about this beforehand. So, the quote for today is, "Passion is energy. Feel the power that comes from focusing on what excites you." That's just what you said.

DC: Yup. You're about to ask me for a quote, aren't you?

CG: I am going to ask you for a quote.

DC: (*laughs*)

CG: Or just make it up! Make it a Diane Conklin quote, you know?

DC: It's interesting because I just found something on Facebook and sent it to a friend of mine. For people who are listening to this who know me, you're going to say Diane is using this word, but it was so true this morning! The quote is this, "Love is the energy of the soul. Fear is the energy of the personality. You must choose between them, moment by moment."

CG: Wow.

DC: I thought that was very powerful this morning. I've been talking to a lot of people in my coaching practice who are sort of letting fear, on one level or another, take over.

I really thought that quote was really kind of cool. Which energy are you pulling from? The energy of the soul? Of love? Or the energy of your personality, which is fear. So I found that this morning.

CG: I think that's a great quote. Why do you think, because I'm noticing it as well, that there are more people approaching what they are doing from a spirit and a place of fear? We can all talk the talk, we can do the "woo woo" thing, right? "Manifest those intentions," and "What you put out there comes back to you." But I am seeing a lot of fear. Do you think it's our economy? Do you think it's the unknown? What do you think it is?

DC: You know, honestly Caren, I think it's just the human condition. And I think it's always been there. But I think it's getting more attention now. I also think that things are shifting in the universe and in the world so quickly now, so fast, that it's a very different time.

I think we can use the economy and those things as an excuse or we can use them as a reason. There is a difference between those two things. I think it's just more acceptable for people to say now, "Wow, I'm a little afraid here. I'm not sure where I'm going," or to admit from a self confidence or self esteem level they don't have all the answers.

Here's the thing, I'll tell you exactly what I told the people I talked to that paid me a lot of money for this advice just yesterday. You don't have to have all of the answers. No one expects you to have all the answers. You're an expert in somebody else's eyes if you're 10 minutes ahead of them. When people come to you, they come to you for a reason, because they already know that you are 10 minutes ahead of them.

You might feel like you're stuck in the mix of it right now, but you have something to give them. You have something to offer them. At some point in all of our lives, in all of our careers, in all of our business lives, we've all had that feeling of "Oh my gosh." We wake up and think, "When is somebody going to figure out that I'm a fraud. That I am making all this up and I don't know what I'm talking about." We all have it. Nobody admits it. People just don't admit it.

I'm here to tell you that I have fears just like you do. We all do, right? It's the human condition. So I think the big thing is to acknowledge it. See where it comes from and then just figure it out. Just deal with it. Everybody has it. It doesn't make you "less than," it just makes you human. So sit with it. I didn't say think about it. I said sit with it a little bit. See what comes to you. See where it comes from. And then, and here's the key, just keep moving forward one step at a time. Don't try to ram the wall or ram your way through it, just lean into the fear a little bit. Just lean into it. Pretty soon, you leaning in, is going to break through it. One step at a time. That's how you get by.

CG: So have you read the book *The Slight Edge* by Jeff Olson?

DC: I have, yeah. I love it.

CG: One step at a time. Little incremental steps moving forward. For those of you who are listening, watching this show, if you have not gotten this book it is on my top 10 must-read… constantly. I have books that I read over and over again. It is a great book and it's right in alignment with what you're talking about.

DC: Yep!

CG: Very much so. Now we have a question I like to ask all of our guests, and you may find it silly, but we've gotten some really interesting answers. That is, if you could spread passion dust anywhere in the world, on anyone in the world, who would you spread it on and what would you hope to accomplish?

DC: You already know what my answer is to this!

CG: (*laughs*)

DC: Wow. So, you know I have a foundation which deals with gay and lesbian, bi-sexual, transgender and questioning youth. And so my answer to your question is that I would go out to any youth, youth in general actually, not necessarily gay or lesbian youth. I would spread it there and my message to them would be very simple. It would be about hope, which is another acronym, HOPE stands for Helping Other People Excel. I think so much of our world is lacking hope today. Especially our kids, our teenagers, our young kids who are getting bullied or they are in that time of their life that they are confused and it's a difficult time and they are trying to figure out where they fit in the world. I would sprinkle that dust there and say to them, "You can be, do and have anything you want in this world. Just have a little hope, get through today and tomorrow will be different."

CG: I love that and I just want to take a little pause right now for anybody who'd like to find out more about your foundation and get involved, how would they do that? Is there a website?

DC: Yup, it's www.dianeconklinfoundation.org. There is a lot of information there, a lot of resources there. If you know somebody who's struggling or is questioning there are all sorts of resources there for them and reach out to us. I would love to talk to anybody who has an interest.

CG: That would be great. Okay, so what song are you passionate about?

DC: Did you just ask me about music?

CG: (*laughs*) I did! At least I didn't ask you to sing!

DC: Now I do have to think! This is really hard!

I have this huge, eclectic music thing, so I guess if I have to just answer this question off the top of my head. This is going to sound really bizarre. This is actually an older song, but I love Pink's *Raise Your Glass*. It is all about celebrating and I think for so many of us don't celebrate enough in our lives. We celebrate birthdays and Christmas and those kinds of things, but we don't celebrate the little victories that we have every day.

Every time we make a sale in the business, every time we get a new client, we celebrate on some level. It might be ice cream out. It might be a bottle of champagne. It might be dinner out. It might be two hours off on a Friday. But we celebrate every single time. So to me, that song is about having a little more fun in our lives. Raising your glass once in a while and getting out there and doing what we really are supposed to be doing, which is enjoying the things we worked so hard for.

CG: Diane, you're reminding me, not that I needed to be reminded, why I like you so much. You've talked about hope; you've talked about celebrating. You're talking about very positive feelings and emotions that I think are missing in so many people today. I want to thank you for that because I'm actually writing down these words, I forget the acronyms right now, but the fact is that you talk about hope and you talk about celebrating those little things. So, so, SO important. I'm hoping that people are watching this and taking this in.

Another passion question. What's your guilty passion… and it's PG! (*laughs*)

DC: (*laughs*) A guilty passion? It's got to be all things sweet. If it's dessert, if it's ice cream I'm going to eat it all. So it's definitely desserts.

It's definitely the sweet stuff in life. It always has been. That would definitely be the guilty passion!

CG: I love that. So we want people to be able to reach out to you and get to know you. I know that you do a lot of things on info marketing, product marketing. You've got some things coming up. Why don't you share with us some of your programs and things that are coming up where people can actually get involved with you directly.

DC: Sure. The best place to go is the main website, which is completemarketingsystems.com. I do a lot of different things, a lot of different programs. October 10th, 11th and 12th of 2013, I'll be doing my big event for the year, which I haven't even decided 100% what we're going to call it. Last year it was called the Marketing Success Intensive. So that will be coming up toward the end of the year. Actually, this weekend I'm doing a 48-hour Info Product Weekend where people are actually going to come in with an idea for their info product and at the end of the weekend they will leave with guaranteed product they can sell for at least $497. So that's coming up.

I have a new program I'm doing on continuity with a former client of mine. I'm actually doing some speaking coming up that I'm pretty excited about. All of those things you can find at completemarketingsystems. com, which is probably the best place to go and stay informed with us.

CG: So there are two places they can check that out. They can check you out at completemarketingsystems.com and they can also go to dianeconklinfoundation.org to find out more about your foundation and to get involved with you. At the end of the day, take an action, guys. Take some action. Get to know Diane. Get to know how she can help you and how you can be in her world because it's a really cool place to be.

Diane, I'm just so happy that you took some time out of your busy day; I know how busy it is. Thank you so much for being on with us today. Any last words that you would like to share with our audience?

DC: I want to say thank you. It's an honor for me to always be with you and share with you. And I mean that sincerely, from the bottom of my heart. I think the big thing that I would like to leave with is the "action piece." Do something. Take a step. Figure out what your implementation plan is. You don't have to do it all yourself. Find people to help you. Be willing to ask for help in your life and in your business. That's how we all do this, right?

Caren can't do this show every week without having people on. When you reach out and you ask for the things that you need, we all grow from that. When you implement and take action, one step at a time - you don't have to leapfrog, that will come later - when you do that, you grow every single day and there is no better feeling in the world than when you push your chair back from your desk and stand up at the end of the day. You're never going to be finished, but to know that you accomplished something. That you talked to someone in that day and it meant something. That's why we're all here. If you do that every single day, it's part of the journey and you're on your way to success, however you define that.

CG: Ditto! Exactly what you said. Diane, thank you for being on with us today. I want to thank all of our viewers. You have many things that you could be doing every single day. I want to thank you for being on with us today and making that choice. Have a great day everyone and we will see you next week on the next episode of *The Passion Point*. See you later.

RACHEL KARU

MAY 7, 2013

CG: Hello everyone, Caren Glasser here and welcome to this week's episode of *The Passion Point*. Every week we interview passionistas from around the world who are following their passion, making a living doing what they love.

Today I am really, really excited to welcome our guest, Rachel Karu. We have been friends now for a little while and she's been on a couple of our shows. I'm really excited that she's coming on *The Passion Point* today because she is going to be talking to us about her passion and how it is she got to where she is today. Following her passion, making a living, doing what she loves.

So Rachel's quest for an authentic, inspirational life led her to create RAE Development, it's a professional and personal development practice. She's an experienced coach, speaker, trainer and singer. We're going to talk a little bit about that singing aspect of it, I love that. With over 19 years of experience, she energizes her clients and creates an affirming environment for personal and professional transformation. I am excited because we have Rachel here today to spread a little bit of her magic with all of us. So welcome to the show Rachel!

RK: Thank you, great to be here.

CG: I'm fascinated by what you do. Especially how you integrate music into your business, and so I want to talk about that. But before we do that we're just going to start by giving the definition of passion. In *Webster's Dictionary* passion is an intense, driving or overmastering feeling or conviction. Would you agree with that or would you have a different definition for passion?

RK: I like that definition and in addition to that, I would say that we FEEL that sense of passion when we are really connected to our values. When we know truly what those elements are that are so core to who we are, that if we are not honoring them then it's like part of us dies. I think in the opposite spectrum, when we're in alignment with our values and we're honoring our values, we get that sense of passion and really being grounded in who we are.

CG: Would you say that you have to have passion in order to be successful?

RK: That's a good question. It all goes to your definition of success. What is your definition of success? If your definition is money, you can obviously earn money by having some strategies in place and you can earn money. If your definition of success is fulfillment, then no, I think you need to be clear about your values; what energizes you, where those passions come from so that you can then take choices and choose behaviors that are in alignment with that.

CG: I love that, and I agree with you, obviously. You have to first define success.

So let's take you all the way back, before you started RAE Development. I know you have a story to tell before you did this. Tell us a little bit about what you did before you started your own business.

RK: Well, my roots are in human resources. Even before that though, my first passion was performing and singing. I went to the American Academy of Dramatic Arts many moons ago. At the time I was a full-fledged perfectionist and I didn't get into their second year program, which was my first big rejection. I just decided in my mind that I had failed. This is it. I suck at this and BOOM! I went to business school.

I actually, ironically, spent a semester as a psychology major. I was the type of person who my friends would always call in middle of the night and I would help them. I also was the diplomat in my family. But after a semester I realized I couldn't really work with mentally ill people, it just wasn't a good fit for me. So I changed to business and I thought it was practical and my parents would be happy. I took my first human resources class on management development and that was it. I was like, "Wow, this is fantastic!" because it had the human side to it.

After college I wound up moving into human resources. I was the human resources manager at BMI music distribution and at that time I couldn't perform, I couldn't sing. Nobody even knew that I had a passion for singing. Then I went on to become the manager, training organizational development at Easton sports, and I was also at Transamerica. I decided to go out on my own after my first day at Transamerica, when they announced a reorganization. Literally, after my orientation! (*laughs*)

CG: Congratulations, right?

RK: It was really bizarre and it worked out beautifully. I wound up staying there for about four months. I could have interviewed for a new role, but by not interviewing, I was actually entitled to a package. I felt like it was a sign from above that this was my time and that's when I launched my business. It's been over 13 years.

CG: So tell us a little about what you do and why you are so passionate about it. Specifically, I know that you have brought music into your coaching. So tell us what that is, because that is just fascinating to me.

RK: Thank you. Yeah, so I mentioned to you that I stopped performing for many, many years. Really what I'm passionate about is inspiring reflection and results. I think so much in our day-to-day we get caught up in a crisis du jour. That we lose touch with what's important to us, what are our values, what it is we are wanting to accomplish. I help people reflect, and reconnect to that important part of who they are, so they can move into meaningful action, and therefore excel. And that's how I came up with the name of my company, which is RAE Development, which stands for Reflect, Act, and Excel.

I am a speaker, a coach, a facilitator, and all of that was going great. But that part of me, one of my values, is around self-expression, it was sorely lacking for me. Even though I was doing it in other ways, that creative self-expression was missing. One day I was actually on my way to facilitate a work-life balance workshop and my life at that moment was feeling way out of balance. I was running late, and I was all stressed and lone behold, BOOM, I was in a car accident.

My car was a mess, I was really grateful that I was okay. But what wound up happening was I ended up going to physical therapy and while I was there, there was a flyer for this workshop called, "Joy of Singing." And I thought, "What the hell is this? Joy of singing?" I did a little research and it turns out that one of the directors was a trainer like me and that intrigued me. I wound up going to that workshop, which is all about facing your fears through singing. After completing it, I started auditioning again. I took headshots and ultimately I started putting on cabaret shows, not just myself, but bringing in other singers and producing shows.

Then, while I was speaking for a CEO association, I told them I was a singer. At the end of the session, they said, "Well, why don't you sing something?" This was all new to me because I used to be very compartmentalized. I would never share anything about my singing, and I did. I sang the verse of a song and they actually sent me some feedback and almost half the members said, "You really should incorporate singing into your presentation."

CG: So Rachel, what was that song that you sang?

RK: It's a John Buchinno song called *Grateful.*

CG: Oh, I love that song! It's one of my favorites! Will you sing?

RK: Wow! (*laughs*)

CG: I love that song!

RK: Okay, you want me to sing a verse?

CG: I do!

RK: Okay! (*closes eyes*) Okay, I gotta ground myself here.

(*sings*)

I've got a roof over my head
I've got a warm place to sleep

Some nights I lie awake counting gifts
Instead of counting sheep

I've got a heart that can hold love
I've got a mind that can think
There may be times when I lose the light
And let my spirits sink
But I can't stay depressed
When I remember how I'm blessed

Grateful, grateful
Truly grateful I am
Grateful, grateful
Truly blessed
And duly grateful

CG: Thank you! I love that song and you sing it so beautifully. Thank you, Rachel. I know that was not fair of me to put you on the spot - no less at 9:30 in the morning, singing! But you just shine beautifully. You need to record that girlfriend! Woohoo!

RK: (*laughs*) Thank you so much!

CG: I agree with the people who responded back to you and said you should put music into your talks and what you do. Did you start doing that?

RK: Indeed, I have and it has been about three years now. Basically what I'll do is integrate usually snippets of songs that tie into the theme of what I'm speaking about or facilitating on. Just as an example, I have a self-resilience workshop that I facilitate. I created an assessment that looks at eight different facets of resilience, one of which is self-awareness. When I define what self-awareness is I sing part of *Defying Gravity*.

CG: (*gasps*)

RK: One of my favorite songs!

CG: That's the song that we start all of our events with! It's that song!

RK: Oh really? That's awesome! I love that!

So that's what I do! Or sometimes I will sing a song at the beginning or at the end that really ties into the theme. Ironically, since the group I spoke to originally and the CEO's that suggested it, they're the one group that actually has not been as responsive or receptive to it!

CG: (*laughs*) Well, you know they played their part in getting you into this space. So for that I'm sure you're grateful that they opened the door. But you know, what do they know, right? (*laughs*)

RK: I think what it's really about, Caren, is back on my message when I sing and that setting is around the power of vulnerability. I use my singing as a metaphor for that and I share with people, "Hey, it's not easy for me to come up and share myself in this way." It's really coming from my heart authentically and you know a lot of people think being vulnerable is a weakness. I really see it as a strength. I am now a recovering perfectionist and as a recovering perfectionist I see that when I let down that shield and I'm willing to be authentic with people, it draws them in.

CG: I just love what you're saying. Also I love the fact that you call yourself a recovering perfectionist. Believe it or not, and you probably will believe this, you are not the first person I've heard use those words. From the extreme of having total adrenal shut down because of trying to live in that space of perfectionism and "you can do it all," to being a recovering perfectionist. I haven't recovered yet, unfortunately.

RK: (*laughs*) It's a life long journey!

CG: Oh my goodness. But you know what? The fact that you've incorporated music into this and that it has helped you in your journey... we've talked about this before, the last time you were on one of our shows, it truly has made me think a little differently, so thank you. I'm a musician, obviously, I sing. Up until the time that you and I met, I never considered incorporating my music into my business world. So I love what you do. And for our viewers who are listening and watching, we're going to give you an opportunity to get in touch with Rachel after this show to find out how she might be able to help you get to that next step or movement in your own business. Maybe music is the answer? Maybe music is the answer for you.

RK: And Caren, if I could, I'd be happy to make an offer to your viewers. I'd be happy to offer a complimentary 45-minute phone session or Skype session to anyone that's interested.

CG: Rachel has graciously, thank you very much, offered to do a 45-minute complimentary strategy assessment call with you. Please take her up on that. I mean, this is very generous, thank you Rachel.

So I have a question for you. What do you tell people when they tell you that they're lost? They're stumbling around out there and they don't know what their passion is. They had it, they don't know where it went, it's gone. How do you help people? Give us a couple tips on how to get back on the road to passion.

RK: It really goes back to what I mentioned before, which is the whole values piece. I really see values as a compass. A way for us to know if we are on-track or off-track. I go through an exercise to help people create a values list and to prioritize that list and also to assess, snapshot in time, how much they're honoring each value currently. Often times when we're in pain it's because we are either not honoring a particular value or sometimes we are overdoing a value.

For example, if achievement is a value of mine, if I were to focus all my attention on achieving, that might then get in the way of me honoring other values like connection or meaningful relationships. Or nurturing myself. So those value pieces are really huge. I also do work on the idea of balance and how to be a more integrated person. So balance is not just how we are spending our time, but what's the quality of that time and living our passion. For me personally, I like singing in my professional world now as a way to experience greater quality of life in different value areas. That helps people as well to identify, "How can I be more of who I am? Not just at home but really be authentic everywhere in all different aspects of my life."

CG: And you very much don't just talk the talk, you're walking the walk. I mean you're incorporating what you're teaching right into how you operate in the world, which is amazing.

I love quotes. Quotes are something that every morning I go looking for something that is going to drive my day. So today, the quote that I put out there is this one… and then I want to know if you agree and if you have a quote that you'd like to share with us. And that is, "Without passion, you don't have energy, and without energy, you have nothing." Donald Trump wrote that. So what do you think about that?

RK: I love it and I actually just last week facilitated a stress reduction workshop which was all around the area of energy. How can we manage our energy through four different domains; the physical, the emotional, the mental, and the spiritual. We're energy beings, so yeah, if we do not have energy in all four domains then we're really depleted, off-track getting sick and having all kinds of emotional problems. So yeah, I totally agree with it.

CG: I admit I kind of knew that you had a thing about energy, which is maybe why I pulled that quote for you. So what quotes do you live by? I know you had a quote that you wanted to share.

RK: Yes! One of my favorite quotes is by Mark Twain, which is, "Dance like nobody is watching, love like you've never been hurt, sing like nobody is listening, live like it's heaven on earth."

CG: Love that. So here's the question of the hour, and I know you're kind of freaking over there, so here it is, if you could spread passion dust anywhere around the world, on anyone around the world, who would you spread it on and what would you hope to accomplish?

RK: (*pause*) My initial reaction was really not one particular person but really the Middle East and the situation over there. Then I thought, well you're talking about passion dust, and as I was mentioning before, I'm a big believer that any strength we have overdone or misapplied is a development area. Any strength overdone or misapplied is a development area. It's great to be confident, but if you're too confident, you're cocky. Great to be trusting, if you're too trusting, you're gullible. Perhaps in the Middle East, both sides of the spectrum are very passionate but perhaps it's overdone and it's an extreme to the point that they are overlooking the greater good. So if I were to spread that dust it would be for them to be able to have more compassion and acceptance on both sides.

CG: Thank you, I appreciate that. Now we were already talking about music and one of the questions I was going to ask is, what song are you passionate about? You've already mentioned *Grateful* and *Defying Gravity*. Is there another one you like that is close to your heart?

RK: Yeah, there's many! (*laughs*) I was going to say *Defying Gravity* but then we wound up talking about it. I don't know if you know the song, *Back to Before* from *Ragtime*?

CG: I do not.

RK: It's a beautiful song. It's all about a woman from the 20's realizing who she is without her husband and recognizing she is her own person. Another one that I really love is *Don't Rain on My Parade*.

CG: Yes!

RK: I combine it with the Barbara Streissand version, you might have heard where she starts with, *Everybody Says Don't*.

CG: Yes

RK: Starts with *Everybody Says Don't* and then goes onto *Don't Rain on My Parade*. That holds a lot of meaning for me. I'm very independent and have a little bit of a rebellious streak. (*laughs*) I just don't want people telling me what to do or how I'm supposed to look or how I'm supposed to pass. Especially in the corporate world. So for me that song is all about being independent and owning who I am. This is me, take it or leave it.

CG: I'm sure our listeners are saying, "We take you, we take you!"

RK: Thank you! I need that! (*laughs*)

CG: You're pretty awesome over there. Do you have a guilty passion that you want to share with all of us?

RK: Oh gosh. Guilty passion... I love to dance! (*laughs*) I take dance classes weekly. They now call them Zumba, it wasn't originally. I had the same teacher but she changed the marketing. For me dancing really gets me out of my head. I like when I'm able to physically connect with the music. And emotionally connect, and really just allow my body to go

73

and get out of my head. Because like many of us, I can be addicted to my brain and dancing really helps me connect to other parts of my body.

CG: It's just that chatter in our heads that just keeps going, going, going and you can't turn it off. Gee! I wonder if I relate to that just a little?

RK: I would say it's a dangerous neighborhood up there and you don't want to be alone there at night in a dark alley. (*laughs*)

CG: I like that. Somebody actually refers to it as the itty-bitty-shitty woman who lives upstairs.

RK: (*laughs*) I like that too!

CG: What would you say is one of the keys to your success?

RK: I think first of all, it was redefining my definition of success. When I first went out on my own, my definition, my ego was so tied to my work and how much money I was bringing in and how many clients I had. Overtime, I really allowed myself and gave myself that freedom and the trust to follow my passion and to reconnect to who I am at my core. Part of that, as I mentioned, was that creative self-expressive person who comes from the heart. I'm practical and I know how to come from the heart. The more that I honor that, and the more that I step into that, I think it has just continued to allow my business to thrive and for me to feel more fulfilled as a person.

CG: That's wonderful. Well okay, so we know that RAE stands for Reflect, Act and Excel. For those of you who have been listening and want to get to know Rachel better and take her up on her very generous offer of a complementary strategy call, please contact Rachel at Rae Development and you'll have a chance to set up a time to chat with her. Any last thoughts you'd like to share with our audience before we say goodbye? I know that you have a lot of things going on. How can they connect with you?

RK: Sure, one thing I just wanted to mention is that I have recently published a book! So if people want to learn more about my journey and consider how they could be taking those lessons to heart, the book is called *Stepping Into More, Lessons from a Recovering Perfectionist.* It can be found on Amazon.com or if you go to my website, which is www.raedevelopment.com. You can find more information there, and of course I'm on Facebook, and Twitter. You just pull up my name, Rachel Karu, and you'll find me!

CG: It's great! I ordered mine already, it's so awesome!

RK: Oh thank you!

CG: I appreciate you being on with us and I want to thank everyone for taking time out of their busy week to watch these shows. We do a *Passion Point* every single week on Tuesday and then it lives out there on the evergreen world forever and ever and ever. So whenever you are finding yourself watching this, thank you for taking time out of your busy day, because we know that you have many, many choices.

Rachel, thank you so much for being with us today. Really it's becoming a habit, having you on our shows. I hope that you will be with us again very, very soon in the future. Thank you for taking time out of your busy day and for those who are listening right now, join us again next week for the next episode of *The Passion Point.* Go on outside today and give somebody an awesome day. Bye everyone!

KELLY FALARDEAU

MAY 21, 2013

CG: Hello everyone, Caren Glasser here, and welcome to this week's episode of *The Passion Point*. This is the show where we interview passionistas from around the world to see what their passions are and how they are pursuing them to make a living doing what they love. Today I'm really, excited because we have an amazing guest with an amazing story, Kelly Falardeau.

She's a burn survivor from the age of two years old. She constantly struggles with her self-esteem and inner beauty. As you can see she is a beautiful, beautiful woman inside and out. She found a way to go from a near-death experience to success. From the "ugly-scar face girl" to the ten top most influential speaker Fierce Woman of the Year, two-time bestselling author and a medal recipient of the Queen Elizabeth II Diamond Jubilee Medal.

Wow! You know you have to ask yourself, how? How did she do this? How did a burn survivor, who constantly struggled with rejection staring, teasing and how did she burst through all of that negativity to create this life of success? You just have to hear her speak and hear her stories to really take her in. Learn and make something of your life in the lessons that she's going to teach us. So Kelly, welcome to Passion Point.

KF: Thank you! I'm so honored to be on your show! I've heard so many good things about your show and I'm really honored to be part of it. Thank you.

CG: Well I'm just happy that you're here. I love doing this show because we get to meet amazing people, like you that are filled with passion. All of us have unique traits and unique passions. So for me, to be able to meet somebody like you and the people who come on the show, it really is an honor and a blessing for me.

We always start this show with a definition of passion. *Webster's* says that passion is an intense driving or overmastering feeling or conviction. That's what passion is according to *Webster's Dictionary*. What do you think passion is?

KF: I believe that but I also believe that your passion is when you are truly following your heart and totally in alignment with what you're supposed to do. I've discovered when I have that passion, nothing can stop me from doing what I want to do. Life is just so full of joy and passion! (*laughs*) I love it. I know when I truly started following my passion, that's when all these truly magical things started happening to me.

CG: Well, you know, the first question that comes to mind when you say what you just did… how did you feel it? How did it feel when you knew it was a passion?

78

KF: Well, you know, you get that vibration in your heart and you can't stop doing it. It's like being Wayne Gretsky, the most famous hockey player and he can't stop doing and playing hockey. You get that vibration and you just want to do it and do it and do it. That's what happened for me when I got my very first professional speaking event. I got off the stage and I was like "Wow, when do I get to do that again?" My heart was just going like crazy and it was like: Okay. This. Is. My. Passion!

CG: How cool is that?

KF: It is!

CG: So Kelly, this show is about you today. Let's take you alllll the way back. Tell us your story. Tell us your journey. How did you turn a crisis into a blessing?

KF: I'm sure when I was little that I didn't know that what I was doing was going to be a blessing, right? But I got burnt when I was two years old. We lived on a farm. We were burning garbage, my cousins were nine and 11 and they were throwing shingles in the fire. A spark came out and landed on my dress and I was burned to 75% of my body. The only thing they said that saved me was that I was wearing a wet diaper.

I spent three months in the hospital. Every second day I had to have surgeries, and then every second year, I would spend a month of my holidays in the hospital, right up until I was 21 years old, for various reconstructive surgeries.

I was always the one who was stared at, I was the one that was teased, I was the one that was rejected, and you know I always struggled with that. I always wanted to be the beautiful girl and I still remember when I was 16, I remember praying at night, and saying to God, "Dear God, please don't make me wake up in the morning. But if I have to, can I at least be scar-less like all the other girls? Can I at least be scar-less so I

79

can be pretty like all the other girls." And that's how I prayed; I was just so tired of being different.

I knew when I was in grade five and I remember seeing a picture and a guy drew a picture of me and it was a circle, with eyes, nose, face, and scribbles all over it and it said, "Scar Face." I saw this picture on my teacher's desk and you know, I wasn't even mad when I saw it, because I knew. I knew I was the scar-face girl. I felt it. I FELT ugly. It just came to a point where I just didn't want to be the ugly scar-face girl anymore. I wanted to be beautiful, I wanted to be hot, I wanted to be sexy, I just wanted to fit in. I knew my scars were never going to go away. But I just had to stop caring about what other people's opinions were of me.

I never had boyfriends because, you know, of course they were too scared of being judged, of being with the ugly scar-face girl. It wasn't until I was 19 that I met my ex-husband and we were together for 24 years. We had three beautiful kids. I lost a baby at 28 weeks and then I ended up having, you know, a set of twin boys, so I have three. My daughter is 14 and my twin boys are 10.

I just stopped caring. I'll never forget, I talk about my garage sale story. A lady came up to me and she said, "They couldn't do better than that?" and I was like WHAT? Like, who are you? I was just like, you know what? I happen to think I look pretty damn good, and I walked out. I thought, "Why am I letting this stranger take my power away?" Why would I let someone who I would never, ever see again make me feel ugly. That was my tipping point. And that was when I said, you know what? I'm not going to do this. Because not once have my friends or family ever said, "Kel, we would love you more if you were scar-less." Not once.

CG: So what did you do? How did you turn this around then? This was your tipping point, so what did you do?

KF: Well you know what? People laugh at me, but I speak about it. I tell how I looked in the mirror and I started to... I quit calling myself names. That's my first secret to self-esteem and I talk about that in my book, *Self-Esteem Doesn't Come in a Bottle*. I basically went to the mirror and I said, you know what? I'm going to give myself permission to feel great about myself.

I looked in the mirror and I realized that I was calling myself the ugly scar-face girl. I still saw all my ugly scars. I looked in the mirror and I said you have big beautiful green eyes. And I looked at them and I said, you know what? I do. Then I would say, I also have a cute little nose! I mean, I love my cute little nose! I would look at the side profile and look: (*turns in profile to the camera*) I've got this cute little nose!

You can't see my ear, but some people would think that it's an ugly ear. You know what? It's me! It's a cute little ear. Who has a cute little ear like that? It makes me unique and different. And then I looked in the mirror and I put on my favorite hot ass jeans and I looked at my cute little butt. I said, you know what? YOU HAVE A CUTE HOT ASS! (*laughs*)

Everybody laughs when I tell that story when I speak, but it's the truth. When I gave myself permission to love all of my little parts, that's when I started to feel great about myself. It was an amazing feeling. I don't have to go tell everybody. I do because I'm a speaker and that's my job, I have to show that level of confidence, but you don't have to do that. You don't have to go tell everybody in the world, you just need to tell yourself.

Start letting yourself believe that you are beautiful. I'll tell you, when I started to look in the mirror the next time, all I saw was my big green eyes, my cute little nose, my cute smile, my cute little ear, and I saw all the parts I loved about me, instead of my ugly scars. And that was what I did!

CG: First of all, what an amazing message that you are telling our listeners and our viewers right now.

KF: Thank you.

CG: Once you got into that space and you were loving all of your little parts… I was just writing notes, love your little parts. Did you write a book called, Love Your Little Parts?

KF: No! I haven't done a book on that but I have a program on it called, "I love your little parts program" So when you go to my website you can sign up for it. It's awesome.

CG: We'll talk about that! So now, you've finally looked in the mirror and your loving your little parts and you're now loving who you are. Tell us what you've done since then? How are you helping people love their little parts too?

KF: Well about three years ago I finally accepted that my passion truly was to be a speaker. I always felt that a speaker had to be a mega person, like Tony Robbins. I felt like I had to be him and I was like, "I'm not him! I don't have that big persona!" I met a lady who was like, "Kel, you need to be a speaker. People would be inspired by your story." And I was like, I'm just a burn survivor, so what? Why does that make me any different than anybody else? She said, "No. You NEED to do it!"

She actually got me to be onstage with her with Joanne Basey and we did like an *Ellen Show*. She interviewed me because she knew I was scared of speaking and all of these women after that little episode, everybody would come up to me and say, "Your story inspired me." After that I took the passion test with Janet Atwood. Janet took me aside and I knew when I did it, my top five passions, one of them was to inspire and so she took me by my arms and she said "Kelly, your scars are your gift. Use them and be a speaker." And I was like, "Fine! I'll do it!" (*laughs*)

Then I took a course by Cheryl Cran and it was a two-day workshop on how to be a keynote speaker. I took some further coaching with her and that's what I do. I speak all around the world to women and teenagers and I also write books. I wrote three books. Two of them have become bestseller books. My first book is called *No Risk, No Rewards*. My second is *Self Esteem Doesn't Come in a Bottle*, and then the third one we just did this November was *One Thousand Tips for Teenagers*.

So it's just been amazing. I just got back in January from Africa. I was speaking over there to burn survivors. It's just been amazing stepping into speaking and I've never had this much success in my life as I do now.

CG: And I'm sure, Kelly, you're going to continue to have even more and more success because you are such an amazing role model; not just for burn survivors but for all of us because scars come in different places and different sizes and shapes, right? It's not always just the physical scars, it's the emotional scars.

KF: Yup.

CG: I'm sure that your story resonates for all of us. We all have scars, let's face it. We all have scars somewhere. I mean none of us are the picture of perfection, nor would we want to perfect.

KF: Right

CG: It's not at all what it is cracked up to be. But you are really a role model for all of us who need to get out of our own heads and stop focusing on the scars. Start focusing on the blessings.

KF: You are totally true. We have this whole perception that we have to have the perfect body in order to be beautiful. That is just so wrong. We put so much emphasis on having to be perfect and having to be beautiful and having perfect hair, perfect makeup, the perfect body, the perfect everything. And I'll tell you guys and girls especially, I've been called hot, beautiful, sexy, gorgeous. Everyday I get called those names and I have the most imperfect body out there! I've got scars all over my face, both my arms, and my breasts are too low. My whole chest is covered in scars. I'm missing a nipple, and yet, I have guys and girls both calling me beautiful. Why is that? I believe it's just because I stopped putting so much pressure on myself to be beautiful for somebody else.

CG: Thank you! Thank you.

KF: I'm trying to be beautiful for me, not for somebody else. And I don't know if you heard about this Caren, but I have a meeting with the brand manager of the Dove Corporation next week!

CG: (*gasps*) Congratulations!

KF: I know! Isn't that exciting?

CG: So Kelly, we are going to have to have you back on to tell us as your journey continues, because that's amazing. But not surprising. It's not surprising like, "Why would they pick you?" It's not a surprise that way. It's actually because your beauty is not just outer beauty. Your beauty is inner beauty and my perspective is that inner beauty is number one over outside beauty. So wow. That's amazing! We're going to follow up with you on that. I'm making a note to follow up!

KF: I know and I'll definitely be keeping in touch with you on that. I'm just so excited about meeting with them. For about three years now I've been wanting to do it but never really had… I knew I had a purpose to call them but never, really knew what it was. Then finally I watched the video that they had put on [*Editor's Note: Dove Real Beauty Sketches*] and I was crying. I finally said that's it! I have to phone Dove! And I phoned them and I just said, "I know I need to connect with you guys

84

on a higher level. I don't know what we're going to do; I just know I need to connect with you." We talked for about a half an hour and he said, "Yeah." So when I'm down in Toronto I'll be speaking at a Women's Conference and I'm going to go meet with Dove.

This is the other funny thing. I'm actually supposed to be at an awards ceremony because I might possibly win a woman of distinction award! But I have to go speak and I have to go to Dove! So... (*laughs*)

CG: You know, I want to say, poor Kelly. All these amazing things, what ever will you do? (*laughs*)

KF: It's funny because my daughter might have to accept the award for me and she also had to accept my Diamond Jubilee medal from Queen Elizabeth. She had to accept that one for me too because I was speaking at another area! (*laughs*)

CG: Well, we should all have those problems, right? (*laughs*)

KF: Exactly

CG: Well, Kelly let me ask you something. What do you tell people who have lost their way? That are just struggling with who they are, they don't know what they are passionate about. What do you tell them? How do you get them back on the path?

KF: I guess the big thing is you have to figure out what is it that you LOVE to do? I even have a whole chapter about this in my *Self Esteem Doesn't Come in a Bottle* book where I talk about how you need to do what brings you joy and not pain in your life. I know many times people have said to me, "Kelly, we think you'd be awesome at selling life insurance. You're just so energetic and you're such a go-getter." And I'm like, are you kidding me? If you put me in that kind of a job, I wouldn't even be able to get up in the morning. Never mind going and talking to somebody about buying life insurance. But if you tell me, "Kelly, we've got a thousand people we need you to speak in front of," I'll be there five hours early!

I think the number one thing you have to discover is what is it that brings you joy. What makes your heart vibrate? Don't do the stuff that's going to make you cry in your office, because that's what I did. I would go to work, I would close my door, and I would cry. What am I doing here? Why am I doing this when I know my passion is to be on the stage or writing books, or doing Google Hangouts with great people like you. (*laughs*) All that stuff is what brings me joy. So you've got to discover, what is that joy.

CG: And then just go and do it.

KF: Do it.

CG: Don't wait. As Nike says, just do it.

So we were talking earlier of how I love quotes. I go looking in the morning for something that's just going to motivate me for the day. Not that I need something to motivate me but just a thought, a praise, a concept, something to keep in the back of my head during the day. This is the one I've come up with today and hopefully you will share a quote or two with us as well. "Excellence can be attained if you care more than other's think is wise, risk more than others think is safe, dream more than other's think is practical, and expect more than other's think is possible."

KF: Oh, that's awesome!

CG: I just love that quote. It's anonymous unfortunately, so whoever you are out there, if you recognize it and send me a note, we'll get your name on it! I love that because it's really just about taking that next step and it's about going for it, going for it all. What's a favorite quote of yours?

KF: I've got a couple. A lot of them are my own.

CG: That's even better! Share your own!

KF: One I just came up with on the weekend. I don't know if you saw on my Facebook, but I had a little bit of a dating disaster, kind of thing. I've been doing the online dating thing, and it's kind of weird for me because I was married for so long. What ended up happening, was the guy wanted me to come to his place and just... you know.. do whatever. And I was like, no, I want to get to know you before that. He goes, "You're not a beauty queen, you know." And I was like "Oh, well." So here's the quote that I came up with. This is the comeback I came up with but I think is going to be a beautiful quote. I said, "You know, you're right, I may not be a beauty queen in your eyes, but I am beautiful in my own eyes and that's all that matters to me."

CG: Love it. I'm writing this down. I may not be a beauty queen in your eyes...

KF: But I am beautiful in my own eyes and that's all that matters to me.

CG: I love that. That's beautiful, and it's so you, right? It is so you and it is your message and good for you. I hope you hung up the phone after that.

KF: Oh yeah! (*laughs*)

CG: And said, "See ya! Next!"

KF: Oh and get this! He ended it by, it was a texting thing, he ended it by saying "and you are going to go…. Nowhere." I just laughed at him. Oh my gosh, you don't even know who you are talking to buddy. (*laughs*)

CG: He totally missed the boat and quite frankly, good riddance.

KF: I'm glad! I'm glad I know that. I didn't waste anytime meeting him because he had a really bad attitude.

CG: Absolutely.

So I like to ask this question of all of my guests. If you could spread passion dust anywhere in the world, on anyone in the world, who would you spread it on and what would you hope to accomplish?

KF: Passion dust on anyone. I would have to say I'd put it on my ex-husband. I would. Because he's struggled his whole life to figure out what it is he wants in his life and he still hasn't discovered what his passion is. I mean it in a very loving way. I really wish that somehow he would discover what his passion is in his life because then I believe he would have more happiness and he would bring more joy to his own life. So it's not a negative thing in any way, it's more of a loving thing.

CG: That's actually very kind of you. Normally people come up with, I'd spread it on all the boys and girls in the world. I actually thought you were going to go in the direction of maybe burn victims or something like that. People that don't feel beautiful.

KF: Well, that's true!

CG: You know Kelly, that's actually very kind of you and I think that it speaks to the person that you are. That you think back on relationships that lasted a long time (24 years is a long time), and that you still have that care of hoping that he will find his passion and be happy. That speaks volumes about who you are. Thank you for sharing that, that was really personal.

So, what song are you passionate about? What song gets you going when you need to get going?

KF: Oh! I have so many of them! I figured out that if I was listening to sappy love songs, I was not getting out of bed in the morning. If I was listening to *I Gotta Feeling*, or all these other high energy songs, all of a sudden, that's what gets me going. So you know of course, my favorite song right now is the One Direction, *What Makes You Beautiful*. I love that, it's an amazing song. Bruno Mars, *Just the Way You Are*, gets me going. Those are two of them. You know I've got so many songs because just before I speak, that's what I've got to do. I have to turn on the music and it gets my energy going, so I love it.

CG: Are you one of those people, one of those speakers that sings in the shower?

KF: I don't sing in the shower. I sing in the car! (*laughs*) My kids tell me, "Shut up, Mom! You can't do that!" But I know the words and they're all, "So what! You're still a bad singer!" And I'm like, but I'm not a bad singer in my own head! Let me sing! (*laughs*)

CG: There's some of that self esteem again. I'm not a bad singer in my own head.

KF: Exactly!

CG: So do you have a guilty passion? Like chocolate?

KF: (*laughs*) Well I did have a chocolate before I came here. (*laughs*) A guilty passion… oh. Hmm. I don't know? Yeah, I do! I do like chocolate. I sneak a chocolate every once in awhile.

CG: Well, we'll just add you to the list with most of the guests that have been on here. Chocolate seems to be running number one on the list of guilty passions.

KF: I wasn't expecting you to ask that! So I didn't have an answer for that one! (*laughs*)

CG: Well I like to throw people off guard. Keep it fresh.

So for our listeners, you can tell that Kelly is just vibrant, she's fun, I mean and she's sexy, and she's beautiful inside and out, and she's funny. For those of you who are saying, I want to get to know Kelly a little bit better, I just got a little taste of her and I want to get to know her better! How can people reach out to you?

KF: The best way is my website. I've got two of them, one is KellyFalardeau.com. The other one just came out in the last few weeks and is HowDoIGetSelfEsteem.net. So we've got some free stuff on there and it's best if you have teenagers. There are some free videos and you can sign up. I think you also can get a free, *One Thousand Tips for Teenagers* book on there, so that's awesome. My books are available up there and of course I'm always looking for more places to speak! That's the big thing for me, I just want to get out and speak more. I really believe that my ultimate goal is to teach women to love their beauty. That's my goal.

CG: There's no question in my mind, Kelly, that's exactly the road that you're on and you're just going to be touching millions and millions of women. I'm just so happy that you were on with us. For the listeners, go ahead and reach out to Kelly via her website or social media. Kelly, any last words you want to share with us before we say goodbye to our audience?

KF: I'm really honored also to be a part of the Day of Love event, that Kelly Frazier is putting on. It's a big live event where we expect to have all these amazing women come to this event. It's in November, so we are going to be having some Google Hangouts about that also. I know you're part of that too. So just reach out, and quit judging people by their looks. It's sad that people think you have to have that perfect body to be beautiful. I'm just living proof that you don't.

CG: You absolutely are. So listeners, just do it. Take the next step, get to know Kelly, and see how she can change or alter maybe your outlook on yourself and life in general. We want to thank everyone for being with us today. We know that you have many choices as to how to spend your time. We're happy that you chose to spend your time with us today. So go out and give somebody an awesome day and we will see you next week, on the next episode of *The Passion Point*.

KIM SOMERS-EGELSEE
MAY 28, 2013

CG: Hello everyone, Caren Glasser here and welcome to this week's episode of *The Passion Point*. This is the show where we visit with passionistas from around the world. Getting to know them and their passion and how they are making a living doing what they love. Today I am so excited with our guest, her name is Kim Somers Egelsee. I hope I said that right, Egelsee? And she is the best selling author of *Getting Your Life to a Ten Plus*. I want that, so we are going to find out how with Kim today.

A multiple award winning inspirational speaker, Kim is a life coach, hypnotherapist, and NLP Practitioner (we'll talk a little about NLP and what that stands for), columnist and TV host. Kim has been a co-host of the global variety talk show, *The Samira Show*, which airs to over 150 million people in Asia, Europe, Canada, United States, and Iran. She also has had her own *Getting Your Life to a Ten Plus* web series with the Hallmark channel's Spirit Clips speaker series. Wow Kim, you have been busy! Your true passion is inspirational motivational speaking, hosting, teaching workshops, coaching, helping others to be happy and empowered, and of course, to be a mom to two great kids. You have a 10-month old, oh my gosh, I don't know how you do all this.

KSE: (*laughs*)

CG: I really don't know how you do all this! People ask me how I do it but my kids are totally grown! You've got a little one, oh my gosh, how do you do all this?

I know that you specialize in getting people's lives to a ten plus. You're helping people discover their life's purpose and getting them to their full positive power with 100% confidence in any interaction. You help people to eliminate stress and fear which can prevent them from moving forward. So Kim, I'm so excited to welcome you to our show. Come on in and say hello to everyone.

KSE: Hi Caren, thank you for having me on *The Passion Point*. I'm excited to be on the show today.

CG: Well I'm exhausted!

KSE: (*laughs*)

CG: I'm totally exhausted reading what I just read about all the things that you do. And so I'm really excited to hear about the many different roads and the journey that you've taken to get to where you are today.

So we always start the show by giving a definition to the word passion. And according to *Webster's Dictionary*, passion is an intense driving or overmastering feeling or conviction. That's what *Webster's* says, what does Kim say? What is passion?

KSE: Passion to me is what my heart tells me. It's an actual physical and emotional feeling I get that fuels me forward and drives me to do what I want to do in a natural way.

CG: How did passion play a part in your journey? Tell us how you got to where you are today doing all the amazing things that you're doing. Tell us about your passion.

KSE: Well interestingly, my background is actually in entertainment. And so that's why speaking has always come natural for me and I know you too, Caren, were a singer. I too did some singing on stage. I did a bunch of things in entertainment, acting, modeling, singing, producing, you name it! So that gave me a lot of experience. I did a lot of hosting and public speaking.

I also went into the field of special education. I worked a lot with adults with disabilities, including schizophrenia. Then I went into teaching children with moderate to severe disabilities mainly in wheelchairs. So I learned a lot about behavior modifications. It's funny, on the side, during all of that, while still doing special education and entertainment, I was doing life coaching! So it's really funny (*laughs*), I was really doing a lot and this was before I had kids!

Taking all of that, my degree was in speech communication. I started getting certifications in NLP and life coaching and hypnotherapy and things that I was excited about. I realized that this is what I'm supposed to be doing. And then a friend said to me, why aren't you inspirational speaking? And she saw in me what I hadn't really seen in myself because I had been speaking all those years. I started to do inspirational speaking, and that's what I ended up being the most passionate about.

CG: Tell us a little bit about NLP, what does it stand for?

KSE: NLP is Neuro Linguistic Programing. The easiest way to explain it is that it is basically brain language programing. I like to describe it in layman's terms as fun, guided exercises that help shift your behavior and your mind to be more positive. So you can shift out of negative beliefs, disempowering beliefs, things that have been programmed. Maybe by a teacher or a parent telling you over and over that you are not good enough, NLP can shift that quickly so that you can start moving forward, in a more empowering way.

CG: Wow. Okay, so that's obviously something good to know. Do all life coaches have that training or is this specialized training?

KSE: No. Some people choose to have it. I like that the best. I love it. I feel like it's very effective. Tony Robbins is someone famous who uses NLP a lot. It just depends on the preference. But no, life coaches don't have to have that. I actually just certified a team of four life coaches that are going to start being on my team and they are Ten Plus life coaches. So they are certified in life coaching but I did not certify them in NLP, although one is certified.

CG: Okay. Now I mentioned in my introduction that amongst the long list that you do, that you have been, the co-host of a global variety talk show, *The Samira Show*. What was that about and oh my gosh, 150 million people!

KSE: (*laughs*) You know I did eight episodes and I actually recently left on good terms. I needed space for something else. It was really exciting and the way it came about was really special because Samira herself is Miss Iran and she found me on Facebook and felt my energy and called me and said, "This sounds crazy, I don't even know you, but I feel like you're supposed to host the show with me." I went down to the set and we just really clicked well together and I was able to bring my own guests on and we did some really powerful, inspiring episodes of the show.

I had a lot of fun and you can see the episodes on YouTube. But there is a lot that I'm doing and sometimes in life it's important to create that space for something new to come in. You get that intuitive feeling that something's coming. So that's what I do quite often, just to kind of make room for new passionate chapters.

CG: I hear you on that! You said you did some education, working with development. Now tell us a little about that, the actual stuff you were doing with developmental education.

KSE: Yes, it's funny, it's ironic my husband actually has a special education law firm and people think that's how we met, it's just a serendipitous coincidence. But I started working with the adults with severe behavior problems and developmental disabilities and so it was very challenging and it helped me in life because nothing surprises me anymore. I mean, I'd be in charge of these adults that would do crazy things like you know, throw all their clothes off and run around the park and you'd have to try to calm them down. You know, just really interesting things and we would work on their behavior so they could be regular upstanding citizens and actually have jobs. So it was a really great job and really challenging and helped me a lot with behaviors of everyone.

CG: I was just going to ask you that! I would have to assume what you learned in that job has really helped you in your coaching.

KSE: Huge! It all correlates and if anything, you don't see the behaviors that severe in day-to-day life. That helped me to put everything in perspective and then I went into working with kids that are in middle school with pretty severe disabilities. Tube feeding and different things like that and lifting them, putting them into physical therapy. And there was a lot of behavior work in that. And so, it did, I felt like it really helped me have a foundation of knowledge of behavior and also the study of educational psychology.

CG: So what do you tell people when they are trying to figure out their passion, trying to figure out what they will do for the rest of their lives? How do you help direct people on that path?

KSE: The first two things that I think are really important. Number one, ask for feedback. I think that feedback is huge. I usually recommend people ask five to ten people that are close to them and maybe even some acquaintances and maybe even posting it on facebook and say, "What do you see in me?" What are the gifts you see in me, what are the strengths you see in me, and very often, more often than not, they are going to see things in you that you don't see in yourself. Sometimes you may even want to ask those people, "What do you see me doing? What do you think my talents are?"

A lot of times something gets fueled inside of you and you realize, "Oh my God, I've always wanted to do that, how did they know?" And that's been really helpful for me in being able to see myself. Like I said, my friend saw in me that I could do inspirational speaking before I did.

Another one is to really think back from when you were a little kid until now, what were you good at? What did you win awards at? And find the commonalities. Don't be scared to do what you are passionate about and make it into a career. You never know! You love planting flowers, you may want to own a flower shop and you maybe are just scared - but why not, you know?

CG: So what I am hearing you say is that when you ask for feedback, it is almost like a mirror. Letting the people in your world, your network, your friends, your family, your connections, act as a mirror of you, to show you who you are possibly. Is that a fair assessment?

KSE: I think so. It's also a combination of being able to get honest feedback about yourself. People tend to think lower of themselves then everyone sees them. Not everyone, but we need to work on that usually.

So a lot of times it is a pleasant surprise, people will think of you way higher and you'll start to see yourself in that way. Or people may have received advice from you or seen you at your best and you didn't even realize how much you helped them. They see these hidden gifts in you. And so a lot of times it is like a mirror and they have your hidden treasures that you're not seeing.

CG: What is your thought process on manifesting intentions? We hear about that all the time, manifest those intentions! Put them out there and like a miracle, they are just going to show up. How do you talk about intentions and goal setting and manifesting things that are positive rather than things that are negative because we are told that our brain focuses onto whatever you are thinking about. What do you think?

KSE: I do agree with that in some ways, but I don't agree in that you are going to think about a million dollars and suddenly it's going to be in the mail. I don't agree with that. I have a formula I use where you have your life purpose. I always tell people, if you don't have your purpose or passion yet, have your passion be that you are working on yourself. You are working on yourself until you figure it out. And that's going to make it come about that much quicker.

CG: So, I'm somebody who loves quotes. I love quotes. In fact, every morning, the first thing that I do is look through my email because I have quotes delivered to my email box. Every week I try to find a quote for this show that speaks to our guest. So I'm going to give you this quote today, it was written by Nancy Coey and she writes, "When work, commitment and pleasure all become one, and you reach that deep well where passion lives, nothing is impossible." Isn't that a great quote?

KSE: Wow. I love it.

CG: Yeah, it's a great quote.

KSE: That is amazing.

CG: I'd like to say I wrote it, but I didn't. I found it, so that's half the way there, right? It's half mine because I found it! So that's a quote for today that I just think was really great and I've already shared it out on social media all over the place. What quotes do you live by?

KSE: I have a lot! My favorite that I wrote is actually kind of cute and fun. It's, "Snails, turtles and clams have shells, humans do not. So take yours off and have the nerve to be yourself!"

CG: I love that! Say that again because I have to write this down!

KSE: (*laughs*)

CG: Snails, turtles and what?

KSE: Snails, turtles and clams have shells, but humans do not. So take yours off and have the nerve to be yourself.

CG: Love that!

KSE: And it's true because, it does take nerve to be yourself. I mean, I think I spent a lot of my life before I felt completely confident trying to live up to what I thought people wanted. And when you finally get to that point where you can feel okay with being yourself... Caren and I were talking and I said, even if I fell on my face while I'm speaking, I can get back up and just laugh at myself and that's just me being clumsy. Just being comfortable in your own skin.

CG: You know I agree with that. Part of what we do on this show and all the different things that I'm involved in (and I know you as well), we just need to be our authentic selves. If we goof up, it's okay, we goof up. It's not the end of the world. Everybody goofs up. Everybody that I know at least, has walked the same path with ups and downs and goof-ups and amazing turn outs and amazing shows. I totally respect that and you living in your own authentic self. I think that is awesome.

So that was one of your quotes. Do you have a quote that you like of somebody else's?

KSE: I love Jim Rohn. Jim Rohn was the first person that I saw when I was 18 and he's really, God bless his soul, but he really has shaped my life. I love the quote that most people know, which is "Work harder on yourself than you do with your job." And that has proven, and then it becomes like the quote you said today, it becomes all one. It becomes like a flowing just YOU. Where YOU are everything. I think that people will realize that if they work hard on themselves, they become the best you, you can be. Life really does become much easier.

CG: I would agree. Those are powerful words.

So if you could spread passion dust anywhere around the world, on anybody in the world, who would you spread it on and what would you hope to accomplish?

KSE: What's coming to my mind on that and I'm really big on intuition and whatever pops in, is that I went to a domestic violence shelter at Christmas time. We delivered gifts to them and you could see the strength deep in these women, but I could also sense the fear that was on top of the strength. I would love to spread the passion dust on them to remove the fear and to let them really go for it with what they really want to do without the fear there. Like just get the fear off quickly and have their full power for their children and for the world. Be examples to the other women that are going through the same thing.

CG: I love that.

And are there songs that you are passionate about? Do you have something that gets you going?

KSE: Oh yeah! My favorite is full of passion! My most favorite artist ever, and I just saw him in concert, is Prince. Every song he's ever done is amazing, but my favorite is *Adore*. If you hear that song, its kind of more of a rare one, but if you hear it, the whole thing just exudes passion.

CG: I'm going to have to go listen to that. I thought you were going to break out into a chorus of *Purple Rain*!

KSE: I love all of them! But *Adore* is kind of a unique one.

CG: I love that.

And do you have a guilty passion? Like chocolate or something that we can talk about?

KSE: Oh! My guilty passion is wine. I will admit it. My husband and I, we love to go to central California and go wine tasting.

CG: Oh, that's awesome.

Okay, so now we are going to get into the nitty-gritty. Do you have some tips or some helpful hints that we can tell our listeners? One or two things that if they just want to get back on the right track, what can we share with them right now that would come out of your tool chest of tricks.

KSE: I think what especially for women, but for men too, one of the things you can do is get rid of the "should's." It's kind of a funny exercise and I actually did it for the first time with this speaker named Neurka, she did it at a workshop and I just felt it was amazing. Make a list of what you feel you're shoulding yourself. It might end up being 100 things. You say, "I should keep the house cleaner, I should be working out, I should eat healthier, I should, I should I should!"

What happens is, that's causing energy blocks and that's causing us to feel disempowered because we put so much pressure on ourselves. So if you actually make the list of shoulds and then you make the decision that you are going to do a ceremony. You either crumble it up or put it in a bowl of salt water and watch it dissolve over 48 hours because that's symbolic to you for letting go of these shoulds. Then you can decide, later, okay I WANT to or I WILL keep the house clean. Or I am feeling passionate about being fit or healthy. That way you are more empowered and you're not holding onto all these shoulds. So that's a big one.

Number two, which is what I'm all about, is connecting people. I genuinely love to connect people and I don't do it to get anything back. I actually recently won an award for connecting at the gratitude summit with Pina de Rosa. I like to meet people and just think, "Okay, who can I connect them with? Who can help them? How would their career be better with somebody in their life (or my life) that we can get together and have a wonderful meeting?" I highly recommend that and I know that Zig Zigler would talk about that all of the time. It's just an amazing way to live and you can give back so much by touching people's lives in that way.

CG: Wow! I love that! That is awesome! Well, I know that you love to connect. You just connected myself with four other women last week. You made a post on facebook and the next thing I knew we are all in a Google Hangout connecting and having fun with each other. So I do know that you don't just talk the talk, you walk the walk. I have to assume it makes you feel good inside because you are doing it for no other reason than to make that connection, correct?

KSE: Yes and it's fun. I feel like it's a puzzle and I know you're the same because I connect Caren with people and she sets up the meeting and so we all do the connecting! (*laughs*)

CG: Well at the end of the day it is these connections that form the relationships which are the fabric of our lives. Without those relationships, I don't think anything else can happen. People are going to buy from people or connect with people that they have created a relationship with.

KSE: Yes.

CG: They're not just going to arbitrarily say, "I saw that person on facebook, I'm going to go buy something from her." No. They are going to create that relationship and when they are ready to purchase something that I might have for sale or offer, then they might come back to me because they have that relationship versus somebody else who they have no relationship with. How does that work with what you do, in terms of creating those relationships and connections, do you find that to be true?

KSE: Definitely true. Facebook actually is very powerful because it leads to things. I guess something like 60% of my business and my connections are on Facebook. One of my friends told me, "You should write a book on Facebook and how to connect on Facebook." It can be so powerful. You know, going to different networking and going to different seminars is great, but I've actually found that Facebook is, if not more powerful, just as powerful. You can meet people in person from the people that found you on Facebook. People come to your events or you'll start to get to know them on Facebook, in fact I think that's how I know Caren. (*laughs*)

You do a nice combination. To me I think it's important to do a nice combination of posts about your business, posts about personal life, so they really get to know who you are. Maybe some great quotes and affirmations and maybe a combination! I like to do combination business and personal posts. For example, recently I did a Tedx talk and I felt a little scared, which I don't usually, and so I did a post. "Okay, I'm really fueled and I'm turning my fear into curiosity and I'm doing a Tedx talk." And just like that, people get to know you. I think that's really powerful.

CG: I agree. I think those are great tips for people looking to use social media as a jumping off place to meet people. I also think that a lot of problems that we end up with is that people will end up staying in that online avenue rather than taking that online connection and meeting offline. If we don't take online and meet offline, we almost live in this... I don't want to say it's a pretend world, we just say, "Oh yes, they're a friend on Facebook."

Have you ever clarified that? "Oh yes! They're a friend... on Facebook." That could mean a multitude things right? I've never met them. They are a friend of a friend of a friend, which is how they became a friend but you don't even know who they are. Or it's somebody that you have had a connection with for years now. I don't know how long you've been on Facebook, but I think I've been on since 2009 or 2010, when it really began to roll out. There are many people that I have in my friend list that I have never met personally, offline, but have met them online and maybe done something of this nature, like a Google Hangout, or maybe on Skype. You know all the different ways you can connect with face-to-face but the mistake I think so many people make is that they never take those online connections, offline.

KSE: Yes, and a big one is go to seminars! There are seminars in your interest and you'll meet great people at those seminars.

CG: Exactly and would you not agree when you meet these great people, and the thing I do when I get back home, is I open my Facebook and I go and friend all of those new people that I just met, right?

KSE: Me too! Yes!

CG: That's taking offline, online, in that case and connecting the two. With the two you have huge power. Huge. So we are so much on the same wavelength.

Tell us a little about what you're doing right now and how people can get to know you better and opt-in to actually getting to know you and maybe working with you. Direct them to where they should go.

KSE: I have a website called kimlifecoach.com and my book just hit number one on Amazon, it's *Getting Your Life to a Ten Plus*. I do in Orange County, for those of you who are near Orange County or LA, I do Willow Tree Women's Circle and now we have men coming too. The powerful thing about that is that there is both business and deep connecting that's going on. The group has been going on for over two years now. It's been very successful and has positive feedback. I have celebrities, experts, authors, and different, really unique people coming in to speak and do panels. We do topics ranging from spirituality to success. So it's a great event to come to and to meet amazing people.

I also have my coaching and I offer one-day coaching with me. Actually, right now, I have a half off special, just for the summer and I only have four spots left. It's basically an all day coaching with me where I help you design your whole life and I consult with you on your social media, on your speaking skills, on different things like that to help you along. Normally, it's $1200 and I'm doing a half-off special for the summer.

CG: Wow. And can they access this through your website?

KSE: They can contact me through the website. The special isn't on there but they can contact me for the special rate.

CG: And how will they do that?

KSE: Through KimLifeCoach.com or go to Facebook and contact me there which is facebook.com/kimlifecoach.

CG: Perfect! Contact Kim to find more information about Kim. Kim, thank you so much for being on today.

KSE: Thank you, It was so much fun.

CG: I was kind of waiting to hear the baby start to cry so we could be totally authentic. Obviously your little one is sleeping through the noise that we just made.

I know that all of our viewers, and we all have many, many things to do with our lives, and we are taking time out today to do this and I appreciate that so much, that you were here with us Kim. If you resonate with the message that Kim has, you really do want to reach out. Just take action! That's the most important thing for all of us! Just do it! Take that next step – whatever that next step is and in this case, take the next step to get to know Kim a little bit better.

As always, we look forward to seeing you next week, on the next episode of *The Passion Point*. Have a great day everyone.

JENNIFER GRANT

SEPTEMBER 17, 2014

CG: Hello everyone, Caren Glasser, here. And welcome to this episode of *The Passion Point*. This is the show where we follow Passionistas from around the world, finding out what their passion is and how they actually make a living doing what they love. And today I am excited about our guest. We welcome Jennifer Grant to our show. She has a passion for serving and supporting others to recognize and embrace that they are indeed truly amazing. This love of life and passion for purpose led her to start her own business, Inspiring Radiance. She now travels locally and nationally as a speaker, writer, and coach sharing the messages, "Lead with Love," and "Your Life is Your Choice," to name a few. Jen's diverse background includes working as an outreach coordinator for a top nonprofit organization; real estate; direct sales; and criminal justice.

Okay, Jennifer, we're going to have to talk about the criminal justice thing, this is something I didn't know about you. She even worked in an all-male maximum security prison, oh my goodness! Jen is changing her life for the better and uses her experiences and lessons to support others to do the same. When she's not supporting others, you might find her walking in nature, reading, practicing yoga, or strapping on her helmet for a motorcycle ride. Her first book, *Dying to be Good Enough*, is due out later this year. And so without another word, I'd like to welcome Jennifer Grant into our interview. How are you today, Jennifer?

JG: Hi, Caren, I'm doing really well. Thank you so much for having me. I'm really excited to be here with you.

CG: Well, I am, if possible, even more excited to have you here with us. I'm excited about your book project; we're going to be talking about that. I do want to kind of digress as well, about maximum security and the whole jail thing and how you got involved with that. That's pretty wild. But first, we're going to start our interview by defining the word passion. Now, according to *Webster's Dictionary*, passion is an intense, driving, or overmastering feeling or conviction. What do you think passion is?

JG: When you were saying that, the first thing that came to mind is it's like the fire within. I feel like it's the fire within us that keeps us going. So when you read that definition, I went yes, that's exactly what it is. For me, it's that fire inside that keeps me grounded and focused forward where I'm meant to go.

CG: So, let's just get to it right now. Where did you discover your passion? I mean, you've been on this journey for a while, let's take you back—let's take you back to when you were a little bit younger or way younger. How did this journey start? Did you start out one day wanting to write a book called *Dying to be Good Enough*? I don't think so. So tell us where you started and how you ended up on this journey and where you are today.

JG: Sure. The bulk of the story, I would say, starts about five years ago. It wouldn't be fair if I said all of it started five years ago, because maybe you remember that picture of that little girl, I think she had blond little pigtails, praying against her bed with her head face down. That used to be me, literally, when I was little. I remember being the little girl praying going, "What is it I'm meant to do?" There's always been this knowing that there's been something in there, and the answer had always been "I want to help people," but I didn't know what that meant. So through a series of events, including a maximum-security prison, it was about five years ago where that journey really unfolded. I was at a specific personal development weekend, when I realized that helping other people meant I had to embrace myself first.

CG: How difficult was that? I mean, you know, we talk about coming into our own radiance and our own brilliance and stepping into our own power. And here you are realizing you have to do that. What does that look like to you?

JG: It was a mess, and it took me a long time. I was 32 years old, and for the first 32 years of my life I had believed what I think society teaches us. For me, it was, 'I'm not good enough, people don't like me, so why even bother.' In those first 32 years, I had gathered enough experiences to feel like I had proved my point: See I'm not good enough, so why even bother. Then at this event, it was actually literally a board breaking experience where I broke through a board, to signify busting through my limiting belief. That's where I finally went, "Wait a minute, if my board can break, maybe there's something more to this." It was at that pivotal moment where life started to change in a really big way. For the first time in my life, I had allowed myself to believe that maybe I am good enough. And then from there, the journey began.

CG: Do you feel that that's a pretty common stream of thought for people to have? I'm not good enough?

JG: Absolutely. Now I can answer absolutely, yes. Prior to this, I would have said there's no way other people think the way I think. I thought for sure I was the only one. Which of course, as you know I'm sure, that's a very common thing. We always think that we're alone in that thought. But the past five years have proved absolutely it. I have not met a person yet that doesn't carry some sort of 'I'm not good enough' in their mind somewhere. Even if it's small, even if we've gotten passed it and healed a lot of it, we all carry it somewhere.

CG: So what was the next step then on your journey? As you realized, you had these limiting beliefs, 'I'm not good enough,' you do this personal development, and now it's five years. Now, you're working towards today. What was your next step? How did you take that next step? And how did you know it was the right step to take?

JG: After that seminar, I decided that I was going to give myself a three-month experiment. What I was going to do is basically, 'if changing my mind about myself and changing the choices about how I felt about me, could it really make a difference?' I would find out over the next three months. And I tell people within two months I quit the experiment, because life had already completely changed. That's when I decided I'm going to start helping other people. I had no idea what it felt like or what it looked like or what that meant, I just knew that I had to share this message with others.

The journey has not been a very straight road; it's been bumps and bruises and twists and turns, but it's been perfect because I just keep following those little nudges that we get, what's the next step going to be? And that's how I got here today. It started with individual people which led to groups, which led to speaking. Once I realized that, "Wait a minute, this really is a collective belief that we all hold," I knew I needed to get the message out in a bigger way. That's what brought me to the book.

CG: Now you're writing this book and it's about to be released and launched. Very, very, exciting. How is that? How did that feel getting all these thoughts and feelings out into writing? It's basically a memoir; it's your story. How did that happen? Was it scary? Was it easy? Did it just like fall out of your mouth, or did you have to muscle it, until you could get to your message?

JG: Well, I think like anything that is meant to be, it's easy once you sit down to do it or actually feel like you have something to share. Then it just comes out. But it was getting to the point of setting aside the time and believing that I have something to offer. Everything that I teach and talk about is already out there, it's not that the message is anything new, it's just my story and my personal story is built into it as well. So was it scary? Yeah, it was scary as hell. It still is, knowing it's going to be out there soon. That's a little bit (or a lot!) of vulnerability. It's very exciting too, because it's been something that for the last two or three years people have been asking me for.

CG: So you know, a question that I always like to ask, because you mentioned the word vulnerability, and that is something I'd like to get your take on. The idea of being vulnerable, that in itself is scary. To me personally, that in itself is scary. That has been the biggest change personally that I've made in my life in the past five or six years is just allowing myself to be vulnerable. How does that feel to you to be vulnerable?

JG: Being vulnerable… there's always that trepidation beforehand, before you release something, before you write something that you know is probably going to touch nerves, before you have a conversation. Whatever it is, there's always a little bit of trepidation. For me, if I'm not being vulnerable, I know I'm not giving everything I can, and I know that it's my responsibility now in order to do that. I see myself as someone who is leading the vulnerability pack because what I've learned is that when I do that, then other women and men can feel permission to feel the same. It automatically gives people a "hey, me too." And if no one is out there doing 'hey, me too,' then we're just sitting back here wondering how alone are we. So I keep looking at it that way, and whenever I put something out there that's vulnerable, it's not about me and what I'm sharing, it's about serving other people so that they recognize, hey, you're not alone.

CG: How has that changed your life now that you've stepped into your brilliance, but not just that, your vulnerability? What is changed now for you now that you've done this?

JG: I think it goes without saying, anytime we talk to people that are willing to be a little bit more vulnerable, that their career expands, their opportunities expand, or connections, and the things that become available to them expand. I would imagine, Caren, you've see that too. As you said you've been doing that more over the last five or six years. Things just expand in a bigger way because people resonate with that. We're at a time right now where people want that vulnerability. They want authenticity, to be candid and from the heart. Whether it's good, bad or indifferent, we need to be sharing that. For me, it's opening up incredible opportunities.

CG: So I have to assume now that you're on this path, and you're writing this book, and you've become vulnerable, and you do a lot of speaking engagements, and you've touched a lot of lives. What do you say to somebody who shows up on your journey and says, "I've lost my passion. I don't know what to do next. I'm lost?" What do you tell them, or do you tell them? Where do you direct them?

JG: It really depends on how much time we have. One of the first things that I would do is remind them how to get connected to their feelings. Because we're never lost; we always have an energy that can guide us, but oftentimes we get disconnected or we fall away from that, not believing that we really have that within. So I would remind them how to get connected with that.

CG: Let me stop you for one minute then. Is there an exercise that you actually can suggest to our readers, just to give a takeaway right now? What would be one way to get more in touch with your feelings?

JG: Yes, you can close your eyes and go through two processes. Start by feeling love. So close your eyes and ask what does love feel like? What does joy feel like? Think of a time when you felt that, when you felt love, when you felt joy, happiness, when you felt alive and vibrant and passionate. Get connected to that feeling. That feeling is your truth. So have that, make a couple notes of it, remember what that feels like.

Do it again, close your eyes, and this time feel the fear side of it. Feel maybe sad, angry, hurt, or disappointed. When is a time you felt guilty about something, and feel how different that feels. You'll feel literally the shift in emotion, the feeling, and the connection in your body.

When we're following a path of light, love, passion, and brilliance, it feels good. I always encourage people to start there. Remind yourself what that feels like, and then go back to what you loved to do as a kid. What lit you up as a child? Or what do you do now where you lose yourself for hours? Reconnect to some of those things, because often we can find that passion within those moments.

CG: Great answer! As we continue along now, we're on this journey and you're finding your passion. Somebody comes to you now and says, "Okay, now what?" I mean, like I'm an accidental entrepreneur, I got laid off from my job or I don't have a job, never had a job or I got fired or there's no work out there. How do you help people or do you help people figure out what their next step is?

JG: That depends on—I think that depends on a couple different circumstances. First of course, we have to make sure we have food and shelter and those necessities. Let's assume that those things are covered and you're in a position to be able to follow this more. Of course, I know that not everyone is. If you're in a position to follow it more and guide into that, I would tell them exactly what I did for myself, which is just take the next step. Too often, we get caught up in having to figure out how it is going to unfold. You don't need to know the how, and most people get lost there. They say, well I have to know the how before I move forward.

No.

Let go of the how, find out why you want this, and then trust that the next step will unfold. For a person that maybe isn't in a position to say hey, I've got all the time in the world, let's say we have someone who's working forty hours a week, and maybe they feel like they're in a dead end job, but they want some more of that passion, they've found something that lights them up. I would encourage them to find how can you add that in your life, even five or ten or fifteen minutes a day. Maybe it's not something full time you can pursue right now, but how can you just start adding it in, and that can be a variety of ways. Of course, that gets back to them connecting with what lights them up, and making that commitment to just add it in a few minutes every day, and that will start leading them closer. Again, they don't need the how, but get connected to that why.

CG: We're always taught that, you know, find your why, the rest will follow. You agree with that statement?

JG: Absolutely. We're told—is it Martin Luther King, Jr.? —who says you don't need the whole staircase to take the first step?

CG: Right.

JG: I think is a quote by him. And that's the same thing. We don't need all the answers. Caren, I could have never told you five years ago that I would be talking to you right now based on this journey unfolding.

I have no idea what's going to be happening in the next five years, but I know that the perfect thing I'm meant to do right this moment is be speaking with you and sharing more about the book and my journey. However that unfolds is perfect, because I'm attached to the why, and my why is spreading that message because I believe it's important for people to know this. What is the 'why' that you want, and that 'how' will keep unfolding.

CG: Exactly. Even our relationship and our connection goes back a couple of years. We met in Minneapolis at an event that we were doing out there, and you were one of our attendees sitting in the audience. If I remember correctly, you were just out of something, and I don't remember exactly what it was, but you were coming to us as an attendee, and you had a lot of things that were going on. That's how we first met, and here we are fast forward a couple years later, and we are connected in multiple ways now because sometimes you just have to let it happen and just let it unfold, the way it's supposed to unfold. How do you feel about that?

JG: I completely agree. I have thought about that recently in fact, as well. I was just coming out of a divorce and a major life transition. I was finding a new home and there were all sorts of things going on. At the time, I wasn't in a position to work together or move forward in certain areas, but again, just keep stepping where I can. And now, two and a half short years later, here we are. Even in those two and half years, life has changed dramatically for me. You don't allow yourself to get bogged down in that stuff. Life will continue happening, but as long as you're still connected to what that 'why' is, the path really will continue unfolding.

CG: Absolutely. So one of the questions that I like to ask my guests on the show is: if you could spread passion dust anywhere in the world, on anyone in the world, who would you spread it on and what would you hope to accomplish?

JG: That is such a beautiful question. I think that might be my favorite. Passion dust. So my passion dust would be called the With Love Passion Dust. And I'm going to pick two groups of people to sprinkle it on, because they're my favorite to talk to. First, I would sprinkle it on women that area 35, 40, 45, 50, 60 and they're in some sort of transition. Oftentimes this is when maybe their children are leaving the house and they are stepping back going, "Now what? Now who am I without these labels?" I would sprinkle it on her so that she starts to realize and remember hey, honey you're amazing, not because you're a mom, not because of your kids, not because of anything, but because you were born. So she would be one person that I would definitely sprinkle that on.

My second group is young women, like high school girls. And I would sprinkle it on them because imagine—I think of what my life might be like if I believed myself even a little bit worthy as a high schooler, how different I might be. Not that I have regrets, I don't regret the path that I've taken, it's brought me to where I am. But giving young women that little boost of 'honey, it's okay. You'll have challenges, yes, but ultimately, you're a gift, and ultimately you're amazing and you have something incredible to offer.'

CG: That is beautiful. I don't know if you know this about me, I love quotes. In social media, I love to put up quotes. Some of them are very, very funny; some of them are thought provoking; some of them I probably shouldn't put up. But I put up things that strike a chord with me either early in the morning or late at night that makes me think. And so today's quote comes from Aldus Huxley from Brave New World, and he writes "I want to know what passion is; I want to feel something strongly." What do you think about that quote?

JG: I love that. One of my dreams, my visions, my great hopes is that everyone can feel a little bit of that passion. Imagine a space, imagine a world where we're all lit up from within. That to me would just be incredible. I love that quote. I'll have to make sure I get that one from you.

CG: I'll send it.

JG: Yeah, that's a beautiful quote. Can I share two quotes with you?

CG: Share as many quotes as you want, this is all about you.

JG: Well I'll give you two then. A quote that I have on my e-mail and it's always in my mind is, of course, Mahatma Gandhi's quote, "Be the change you wish to see in the world." I lead myself forward with that. I see that every single day. I make sure I look at it every single day, so that I remind myself to step back and step into that place. Who is it that I want to become and how do I want to do that, how do I want to support that change and growth going forward.

The second one is Marianne Williams and *Our Deepest Fear*. It's quite long, I won't give you all of it. So look that up, *Our Deepest Fear* by Marianne Williamson. She talks about our deepest fear is not that we are powerful, our deepest fear is that we are powerful beyond measure. It's so telling and so incredible to me. The words, "as we let our own light shine, we unconsciously give other people permission to do the same." That goes back to what we were talking about with vulnerability too, it's letting that light shine. As we do, we remind others that they are also of that light and they also have that to shine. So that would be my other favorite quote.

CG: Well, I like both of them, and thank you so much for sharing them. I want to talk a little bit about your book, because it's about to be launched like any day.

JG: Yeah.

CG: It's called *Dying to be Good Enough*. Can you give us just a little idea of what this is about and how it came about?

JG: *Dying to be Good Enough* and then my subtitle is *A Journey of Acceptance and Discovering Ultimate Love*. So growing up I had always, as I said, I was always kind of a seeker, looking for what it is I'm meant to do. Meanwhile, parallel along that journey, I had always run into moments or obstacles, people telling me things that had reminded me, "you're not good enough." So I remember growing up always trying to be good enough. I had always wanted to hear these words from anybody that I talked to, my mom, my dad, siblings, friends and family. Anyone that I'd talked to, I had longed to be good enough for them. So that was always part of the journey. This book is part journey, part stories, part my experience built in with these lessons that for the past five years I've been putting into place in my own life and sharing with other people.

So it's *Dying to be Good Enough: A Journey of Acceptance and Discovering Ultimate Love* because as we know, life really is a journey. Where I am today is not where I'll be in ten years from now; and where I was ten years ago is not where I am today. Life is always a journey. That ultimate love, for me, is the love that I can give myself, because I feel like that is the hardest love for us to offer. It's easy to love our children, it's easy to love our friends, it's easy to love our family and other people, but it's the hardest to love ourselves fully and completely. So this book is all about my story and lessons that I share with other people along this amazing journey we call life.

CG: I love that. I know that people are going to be able to go to Amazon; they're going to be able to go to bookstores and order your book. I mean, it's going to be available all over, and they can also go to your website, I know, to find out more information. What is your website that we can let our readers know?

JG: Sure. The website is www.inspiringradiance.com, and you can find me there. I love people finding me on Facebook, so reach out to me on there. www.Facebook.com/inspiringradiance and e-mail me directly, all of my contact information is on my website. I am the type of person—and maybe this will change in five years if I'm too busy—but I'm the type of person who loves connecting with people individually. So if someone e-mails me, they're going to get an e-mail response from me. I don't have any little box in the background handling things. Personal connection is perfect for me.

CG: I love that. Any last thoughts that you want to share with our readers before we finish up our show today? I'm just so fascinated by your journey and just because I've been a part of it for even a short few years. I'm so excited to see where you're going and who knows where you're going to be in ten years, quite frankly, as you said. I mean, you just don't know. But I love the fact that you are fearless and that you are just perpetually moving forward, which is an awesome thing, and I think a great message for our readers. So any last thoughts or messages that you would like to share with us?

JG: Oh, my goodness, there's so many things I could say. But I think the thing I would say, that I would say to anyone if given the chance, is know that you're a gift. Know that you're here for a purpose. Know that you matter and your voice counts. It's up to you to decide to make that choice to live from that place.

CG: Amen to that. Thank you so much, Jen, for being on the show today. I so appreciate you and you taking time out of your busy day to be with us. I want to thank our readers because we know you have lots and lots and lots of choices as to where you spend your time. We are so appreciative that you've chosen to spend your time with us today. As we always say at the end of each show, we can't wait to see you next time on the next episode of *The Passion Point*. Have a great day everyone. Bye-bye.

Passion Playlist

Life by Beckah Shae

Walking on Sunshine by Katrina and the Waves

Celebration by Kool & the Gang

Don't Stop Thinking About Tomorrow by Fleetwood Mac

Better Days by Eddie Vedder

Raise Your Glass by P!nk

Grateful by John Bachinno

Defying Gravity from *Wicked*

Back to Before from *Ragtime*

Don't Rain on my Parade by Barbara Streissand

I Gotta Feeling by Black Eyed Peas

What Makes You Beautiful by One Direction

Just the Way You Are by Bruno Mars

Adore by Prince

About the Author

For the past 30 years Caren Glasser has dedicated her personal and professional life to communicating and connecting with people. Her past experiences have allowed her to meet many different people and make a difference in their lives. In the early 90's she was a children's rock and roll singer, signed with Rhino Records. She traveled the country singing songs of self-esteem. That experience culminated with a concert at Carnegie hall. During that same time she owned a creative arts company that provided programming for the public and private schools sector in Los Angeles. She has learned a lot about what it takes to create positive experiences in our lives. Today, as the founder of Promote Your Passion™, she focuses on helping people find their passion and create better lives for themselves.

www.ingramcontent.com/pod-product-compliance
Lightning Source LLC
LaVergne TN
LVHW021354080426
835508LV00020B/2281